WITNESS OF A FRAGILE SERVANT

OF A FRAGILE SERVANT

*A Personal Look
at Pastoral Preaching*

CHARLES B. BUGG

Smyth & Helwys Publishing ©2003

SMYTH&
HELWYS

Smyth & Helwys Publishing, Inc.
6316 Peake Road
Macon, Georgia 31210-3960
1-800-747-3016
©2003 by Smyth & Helwys Publishing
All rights reserved.
Printed in the United States of America.

Library of Congress Cataloging-in-Publication Data

Bugg, Charles
    Witness of a fragile servant: a personal look at preaching /
    Charles B. Bugg
    p. cm.
    ISBN 1-57312-389-7 (alk. paper)
    1. Preaching
    2. Sermons, American–21st century
    I. Title

    BV4211.1 .B84 2003
    251–dc21

                                                2002152657
                                                CIP

Table of Contents

SERMONS

To Diane, whose love for God, love for others,
and love for me have inspired me
more than she will ever know.

Introduction

While I'm not quite ready to be taken out of the ball game, I realize that I'm well into the second half of my active ministry. Recently, I had a birthday and understood again that when it comes to age, we count up and not down.

I turned fifty-nine. I'm at a point in my life when I'm active, healthy, able to teach what I love, part of a wonderful seminary community, and preaching every Sunday but don't have to attend deacons', finance, or personnel committee meetings anymore. To all the laypeople who attended those meetings with me throughout the years, I like you—but I wish we could have spent our time in a different venue.

I'm also getting more reflective as I get older. I'm trying not to be obnoxious about it. I don't ask my family to sit and listen to old preacher stories, but once in a while I find myself talking about some past event and saying, "What did you think about what happened?"

Because I love preaching and I love the community of faith we call church, I decided to write this book on "pastoral preaching." The only way for me to write this kind of book is from a personal perspective. That's why I've titled it *Witness of a Fragile Servant*. You will see in the book that I'm the "fragile servant." You will also see that I've not touched on every component of pastoral preaching. I've tried to make this more than a "how-to" book. In sharing some of my brittleness, I hope to help and maybe offer a learning experience to some of my colleagues in the ministry.

I want to express my appreciation to people who have called me to be their pastor. While my résumé includes names of churches, I always think of the *people* in those churches. Even at the student church I left thirty years ago, people like Elmo Chasteen and Cora Etta Henry were church to me and to one another. What a privilege to have people who allow you into their lives, who come to know your strengths and weaknesses, and then give you the opportunity to say a word to them each week.

I want to thank ministers I've come to know. All of us who are ministers need someone to listen. I've had those who have listened to me, and I've tried to listen to others. You have to be called by God to be a pastor. The pastorate is a demanding profession requiring a multiplicity of gifts and the ability to see both praise and criticism in proper perspective. Often, pastors don't see the results of their preaching and their ministries, so the call to be a pastor requires someone who knows within herself or himself that she or he is making a difference. However, the church is the most critical place in the formation of people's faith. My prayers and appreciation go to those who labor, often without much recognition in the place where God has called them.

I also want to thank those who have been my students through the years. Sometimes, I don't even know why I call them my students. In more instances than they realize, they have become my teachers. Several times each year I try to schedule occasions where I can preach in a student's church or go to be with my former students. They make me so proud. They are committed to the ministry; they care about people; and their skills in ministry are encouraging to me.

Those who know me understand that my typing and computer skills leave much to be desired. I have promised my children, who are thoroughly embarrassed that their dad still uses legal pads and a pen, that I will address my "computer-challenged" status as soon as I run out of my collection of legal pads. What Laura Beth and David don't know is that I have enough pads stashed away to make it to the end of my career. But I do want to thank Laura Beth, my daughter, and Stephen Cook, my teaching assistant at Baptist Theological Seminary, for taking bad penmanship and transforming it to hard copies and to disks.

Finally, I want to thank my family. I've saved the best for last. Laura Beth and David have brought me enormous joy and pride. Laura Beth has picked up the theological mantle and is in the process of writing her doctoral dissertation at Harvard Divinity School. She has brought a new member to our family, her husband Bryan Gaensler. Bryan is an astrophysicist who comes from Australia. His favorite sports are cricket and rugby. Knowing virtually nothing about cricket and rugby and having taken the minimal science requirements in college, I haven't tried to engage Bryan in any deep conversations about work and sports. However, he's a bright, compassionate young man whom we have learned to love.

I have written before about our son David. In 1983, he was diagnosed with a malignant brain tumor. Fortunately, David's tumor was treatable, but the lesion, the surgeries, and the radiation treatments have left David unable to function in certain areas. David lives with Diane and me, and each day we come to appreciate his kindness, his sensitivity, and his love for sports, which he shares with his dad.

Diane, to whom this book is dedicated, is more than a wife or a spouse. I'm a better person just for having known her. Across the years of marriage, my love for all that she is has grown. In every way, Diane has encouraged me to use whatever gifts for preaching and ministry I may have.

I've already said "finally," but the letter to the Philippians has two of them, so I'm in good company. Thanks to those who read this book. I pray for all of us, that our days are rich with a sense of God's presence.

A Word from a Fragile Servant

Forty-three years ago I preached my first sermon. My listeners through the years have varied widely. Some of my first sermons were spoken to men in a rescue mission and to prisoners, where the only sound I remember was the prison door slamming locked behind me. I've spoken to young people at rallies and to college students in chapel. I continue to preach periodically at nursing homes and assisted living facilities.

In fact, one of my fondest recollections was speaking at a one-night revival at the Eastern Star Nursing Home in Louisville, Kentucky. I was teaching at the Southern Baptist Theological Seminary. A young woman in one of my preaching classes was compassionate and caring in addition to being a gifted preacher. She served as chaplain at the Eastern Star Home. "Would you preach a Saturday night revival for us?" she asked me one day after class. "The women want to have a revival service. They want to sing some of the old, familiar songs. They want to remember when they were younger and revival meetings were the times when people were refreshed and renewed. The women will be dressed in the best clothes they have," my student said. And they were! What a night to remember—not so much for what I said, but for what they said by their presence and shared through their recollections.

I still laugh when I remember the white-haired woman in the blue silk dress and matching hat who told me how much she liked my preaching. During the service, she sat near the front, and I noticed she slept soundly through the whole sermon. "You're a good preacher," she said as she left, and I simply thanked her. Those of us who preach have learned to accept compliments whenever, wherever, and however we get them.

Thus, in the years since I first felt the divine nudge to preach, I have spoken to people in different places who exhibit different degrees of alertness. However, most of my preaching has been in the context of a church. Some of these churches have called me to be their pastor. What a wonderful and overwhelming experience. As a pastor and preacher, you live into the lives of others, and their lives live into yours. You know their stories, and they know your stories. As a pastor, you realize that Augustine, the early church father, was right when he said the most critical component in "sacred rhetoric" was the "ethos" of the speaker. People in the church come to know our character. While the congregation hopefully listens to our *words*, they really listen more to *us*. Only the truly neurotic listeners demand perfection from their pastors. However, the folks in the church have every right to expect that their minister is ethical, caring, and prepared, and to trust that the message the preacher shares is also critical to their own lives. How sad to see a church that distrusts its minister. Eloquence is no substitute for ethics. Words well spoken are undermined by a life poorly lived.

Sometimes, I have preached as the "interim pastor." As a little boy reminded me, that's like being the preacher until the church can get a "real preacher." While you're not the real preacher, you still care about the people and want to speak in healing and helpful ways. Why did the former pastor leave? What was the pastor's relationship with the congregation? Is the church glad he or she is gone? Are the people sad? Are some of the congregations glad, some sad, and some angry about what may have been said or done to provoke the minister's leaving? How does the church feel about itself? Like individuals, churches have images of who they are. Some congregations may see themselves as divided, troubled, and unworthy of a really capable minister. As a seminary professor, I have served different kinds of congregations during the time between the leaving of one pastor and the calling of another. While each situation differs, I find that many churches need a better self-image. It's not that they resist doing what a church should do. Like some of us at times, the self-image of the congregation is so low that whatever energy the church has is spent trying to survive. One of the best gifts any minister can give a church is to call it back to remember its identity as the children of God and to become more empowered in the process.

I have preached as a pastor. I have spoken as the interim pastor. I also find myself doing quick excursions into various churches. These times of proclamation go by different names. Sometimes, a church wants a series of revival or renewal services. Often, these times of preaching are tied to particular seasons of the Christian year. In my religious tradition, more churches are recognizing the necessity of preparing their members for the experience of the pivotal days in the life of faith. For many years, most Baptist churches shied away from spiritual preparation for times like Christmas and Easter. Now, it's not uncommon to find congregations that take seriously the seasons of Advent and Lent as periods of preparation for the observance of the critical days of Christmas and Easter.

Obviously, these short trips into the life of a church present unique challenges for preaching. As a preacher, you don't have a relationship with the congregation. Most of the listeners don't know you except through a few facts on a résumé, and while we as preachers may try to get as much information as we can about the church, we really don't have a personal relationship with them. The distance between the speaker and the hearer is large. We haven't had a chance to know and to be known, to listen and to share those stories that have shaped us.

Interestingly, this type of preaching serves to remind me of something I am prone to forget. In the final analysis, effective proclamation is a mysterious transaction. It's mysterious in the sense that people's lives are changed not by the clever adjustments or relational skills of the speaker, but by the God who knows us all and in whose name we come together. In many ways, this recognition that the effects of preaching reside in the God who gives life to our words has freed me from anxiety.

Still, I want to know as much about the congregation as I can. When I preach, I want to project a sense of my caring for the church and empathy for the common burdens that we bear. At the same time, the recognition that God works in the words of the stranger frees me from the compulsion to do too much in too short a time. This compulsion may tempt a preacher to turn into a pseudo-entertainer. Maybe I'll tell them a few jokes to warm up the crowd. Then I'll tell the folks how glad I am to be there. Of course, I have to talk about the church's pastor and how blessed the congregation is to have him or her. What's really going on in this kind of endless introduction? Understand that I'm not saying a few kind words aren't appropriate. I am the church's guest. I am glad to be there. Most of the time, I like the pastor and want to affirm his or her ministry. However, when this kind of "getting to know you" goes on incessantly, it becomes counter-productive. Unintentionally, it communicates that the congregation won't hear the words of the sermon unless the guest minister ingratiates himself or herself to the listeners. What we do as preachers is assume that people won't listen to what we say unless they know us and presumably like us.

While being nice, caring, kind, and gracious are admirable virtues, this kind of meandering preamble indicates that the sermon itself has little power apart from those of us who present it. The engaging manner of the preacher becomes more primary than people's being engaged by the Word itself. Perhaps this phenomenon is partially a result of the emphasis ministers have placed on the element of "delight" in preaching. We have taken effective strategies such as storytelling or self-disclosure to extreme limits. Instead of story or disclosure serving the interest of the message, they become devices to make the preacher more likeable or more known to the listeners.

I share this because I know that one of my strong desires as a preaching minister is to be liked and affirmed. While I certainly want to say something meaningful, I also want to say it in such a way that the listeners will think I am an effective communicator. While the desire to be well received by others is probably part of the make-up of many of us in the ministry, it can also become our undoing. The pastoral ministry itself is an overwhelming vocation. Think of the expectations others have of us and we have of ourselves. Now think of the inevitable distance between the ideal and the reality of what we are and what we can do. Not only do we endure the negative criticism of those who don't believe we measure up, but also, and perhaps more significantly, we are hard on ourselves because we recognize our imperfections.

A student who had been in the pastoral ministry and left because of his frustrations shared his pain with a group of fellow ministers. This minister had entered his first pastorate with the best intentions. A few years later he left the church vowing never to return as a pastor. In retrospect, he understood that he had brought some of the criticism on himself. As the church situation deteriorated, he became less motivated to prepare sermons or to fulfill his parish responsibilities. Anxiety and depression became his constant companions, and he talked movingly about the distance he felt between what the church represented and himself. At the moment when he needed the resources of his faith, he experienced the aloneness that comes when we feel uncertain or unloved by God.

To his credit, this insightful minister didn't blame all of the problems on the church. He knew he had made mistakes. He understood that he had said things that probably should not have been said. He acknowledged that at some point he had lost his focus and was looking for some acceptable reason to leave the church. At the same time, those of us who listened to him understood that he wasn't solely to blame. The church had not been clear about its expectations of him as a pastor. Several influential people who didn't care for his laid-back style as a person and his low-keyed way of preaching made their opinions widely known. Unfortunately, as so often happens, no one made attempts to effect reconciliation or to make the separation as gentle as possible. The result was a messy divorce. He was hurt, and I believe that the church was also wounded because it didn't face some of its own issues.

However, what struck me most in my conversation with this student was how he described the image of himself as a minister. He had left the seminary as many of us do: filled with enthusiasm, he was going to be the fearless prophet calling the church to mission. At the same time, he would be the faithful pastor walking with parishioners through the broken places of their lives. "I saw myself," the student said, "as a change agent."

At that moment, I became less a teacher and more a fellow traveler. That is precisely how I had seen myself for much of my own pastoral ministry. When I left the seminary, I wanted to help the church. I wanted to be the best pastor I could. In a word, I loved the church. However, that love was mixed with my own fear. What if I failed? What if I threw away all those years I had invested in education and wound up selling life insurance?

Well, the good news is that I'm not in the life insurance business. Filled with love and fear, I have stayed with the church, and most of all, churches have stayed with me. At one level, I believe most of my ministry has been a success. As a pastor in our denominational system, I rose through the ranks, continuing to go to larger churches, which, right or wrong, is often regarded as a measure of success. My preaching seemed to be well received, and my generally extroverted personality helped me relate to a wide variety of people. Since I'm well organized, I was able to do the administrative tasks of the church and to budget my time among the required tasks of a pastor. Perhaps, most importantly, I have a wonderfully supportive family. My children seldom complained about any expectations of them, and the churches where I served were thoughtful not to place unnecessary burdens on them. My wife, Diane, has been a wonderful colleague and companion. She is an extraordinarily compassionate individual who found her place in each church and who never felt constrained to play a "role." Diane has always had the wonderful ability to be comfortable with herself and to be loved by others for the considerate, caring person that she is.

But back to the younger minister's comment that triggered so much anxiety in me. "I left seminary," he said, "with the idea of being a 'change agent.'" So did I! I look back at the whole stretch of my life and see that for as long as I can remember, I've wanted to "prove myself" and live up to my own perfectionistic expectations. Perhaps some of this stems from my own nurturing as a child. Someone has astutely observed that children are keen observers but poor interpreters of what they see. Although intelligent, neither of my parents finished high school. My dad became a mid-level manager at Pan American Airways in Miami. My mother stayed at home until I was older, when she began to work as a cashier in a department store.

I was born in December 1942, almost six years after they were married. I was their only child until my brother was born eight years later. My earliest childhood memories are sketchy. We moved several times within the city of Miami. That meant new schools, new neighbors, and new people to introduce myself to as Chuck Bugg. I dreaded the first day in a new school. When the teacher asked us to introduce ourselves, and I said "Bugg," you can imagine the laughter. I wish I had a quarter for every time somebody asked me, "Does anybody bug you about your name?"

However, what stands out most in my memory as a child is my dad's drinking problem. I knew nothing about the dynamics of alcoholism. All I knew was that my dad would often arrive home late from work, and when he came home, his speech was slurred, and he staggered as he walked. As I got older, I wondered if the neighbors knew the secret that we never talked about in our house. While my father never physically abused us, I remember a growing sense of shame about our family's secret. I also recall deep anxiety about how my father would act. When he was sober, he was a good and kind person. When he was drinking, however, he acted in bizarre ways. For example, when I was about nine or ten years old, he became convinced that a burglar was in our house. He awakened the rest of the family early in the morning. Holding a baseball bat, he led us room by room through the house looking for the burglar. At the time, I recall thinking, "This is absolutely idiotic. Nobody has broken into our house." By the way, we never found the intruder and never found evidence that anyone other than our family was awake at that ungodly hour of the morning.

When I was twelve years old, my father stopped drinking largely through the efforts of people from Alcoholics Anonymous. The local Baptist church became the center of our family's life, and we thrived among people whose names I remember, such as Bob Payne, and others whom I knew only as "Brother Baker" and "Sister Miller." Whoever all these folks at West Flagler Park Church were, they loved me and encouraged me to develop the gifts I had. While this church was far from perfect, the folks helped me to see what a group of people called church could mean to somebody. They loved my family and me into a vibrant faith in the God of Jesus Christ and gave me an everlasting appreciation for the church.

While this church helped give me a new perspective on life and a new confidence for life, they couldn't possibly eliminate some of the effects of my earliest childhood experiences. What has stayed with me the most has been the chaos I perceived and how little I could do to control the world around me. My response was to become the "good child." I did well in school, was elected by my peers to positions of leadership, and at least for a time thought I was a good athlete. Even in elementary school, I regulated my schedule so that my homework was always done before I went outside to play. Though I dreaded those late afternoons when my dad would come home drinking, I learned how to adapt and knew when it was better to stay out of the way. From my perspective now, I look back to see how my situation affected my ministry and even my preaching.

On the more positive side, I do have compassion and care for people. I did find areas where I could achieve. I am highly organized and have no problems with time management. In preaching, I try to convey empathy with people and approach my sermons with the attitude that we are all in some way "fellow strugglers." Despite the fact that churches can be dysfunctional, I have maintained my deep love for the church and my commitment that through its sermons, hymns, prayers, practices, sacraments, ordinances, and outreach, the church can still be an agent of redemption and reconciliation.

However, the same event in our lives that gives some light also casts its shadow. For most of my life I have struggled with what it means to be loved by God and accepted unconditionally by the Gracious Other. Henri Nouwen wrote so beautifully about being the "beloved" of God. In his own way, Nouwen seemed to write about this love more clearly than he ever came to know it himself. I can identify. Listeners who tell me that I make the grace of God so clear to them probably have never known how many times I have wanted to live more out of my own message.

Preaching as a pastor, this has often resulted in the desire to preach sermons that are well received and to be recognized as an effective communicator. In the words of my student, I have wanted to be a "change agent." I have wanted everything and everybody to be different because of my words. You do recognize the "codependency"? As a pastor, I have

assumed responsibility for others and for myself and have become frustrated
when we're not all growing in a straight line to be more Christlike. At a con-
ference, Tom Long, that wonderfully gifted homiletician, reminded us about
the church father Augustine and his desire for preaching. Baptizing the work
of the Greek philosopher Cicero, Augustine stated that the intent of a
sermon was to teach, to delight, and to persuade. Long pointed out that
these elements represented an appeal to the mind, heart, and will. Then, as
he does so well, Long humorously remarked that the ideal response any
preacher could receive after a sermon was, "Your message taught me something; I was moved by it; and I intend to act on what you said." All of us in
the room laughed because we had never received the ideal response.
However, I was crying on the inside because that's what I've really wanted
every time I've preached. I've wanted to be the change agent. I've wanted all
of us to be right with God. In effect, I've wanted what Jesus never achieved
with his preaching and teaching.

While I still want to be an effective preacher, I'm coming now to try to
re-vision myself and my preaching. I've spent much of my life trying to get
other people's approval. This hunger for acceptance is never filled. For a
moment, there's the "rush" that comes when somebody says a complimentary word. But the vacuum is soon back, and you wait for somebody else to
make you feel good about yourself. As a preacher, this creates enormous personal anxiety and has the potential for turning preaching into a manipulative
exercise designed to get the appropriate response.

Now I'm trying to see preaching not as a way to get something but
rather a way to give something to God and to others. We want to give our
best, but our best may simply be what we are able to give most sincerely and
authentically. My wife has taught me much about gifts. Recently, I passed a
kiosk at a shopping mall. The vendor was selling crafts. I bought one that
said, "I Love You!" It cost me all of $2.49 plus tax. When I gave it to Diane,
I was amazed at her response. "This is better than a $3,000 diamond ring
because you thought about me." I'm not going to argue the point. My mari-
tal stock jumped considerably because of $2.49 plus tax. I'm certainly not
the most thoughtful husband in the world, but I did buy that craft because I
love Diane, and I was sincere. I wanted to give her something!

What if we saw preaching this way? We are pastors. We have much to
do. However, we love the people to whom we speak because for all their and
our idiosyncrasies, we are children of a loving God. We are not preaching to
get them to like us or even for them to be conformed to the image we have

of what they should be. We know words are powerful, but we trust any changes that happen to the God who changes us if we are open. We are not change agents. We are lovers, givers, people who bring our offering of the sermon and let God have God's way with our words. We are servants. Who knows what will happen? What we know is that we are not in control.

Our offering to God

The Need to Care for Ourselves

Many of us have been touched deeply by the life, ministry, and writings of Dr. Wayne Oates. Wayne Oates was one of the pioneers in the pastoral care movement. His influence on students is legendary. Listening to Dr. Oates, I thought everything he said was just a little less inspired than the Bible. When I returned to Southern Baptist Theological Seminary to teach preaching, I served for a time as his interim pastor. I would think, upon seeing him in the congregation, "Now what can I bring to his life that he doesn't already know?"

There I was, walking into the pulpit at the St. Matthews Baptist Church in Louisville, Kentucky, and in the congregation sat Wayne Oates. For me, this was almost like preaching to God. What do you say to God? God already knows it all. What if I confused the text or came out with some statement that revealed my total lack of understanding of the human psyche? Would Dr. Oates slide down in the pew, then slither out of the sanctuary after the benediction as he mumbled, "Chuck was in my class, but I don't claim him"?

What I discovered, instead, was what I've found in truly gracious people. Each Sunday, Wayne and Pauline Oates would take the time to see me after the service, and with those wonderful smiles, would thank me for something I had said. I'm not presumptuous enough to believe that I taught Dr. and Mrs. Oates many new things. However, preachers well understand when I say, "A kind word from these two people would carry me all the way to Thursday afternoon."

Actually, when I looked at this incredibly thoughtful man, I remembered and was grateful for all the wisdom he had imparted to me as my teacher. I don't even recall whether I heard a particular piece of advice in his class, read it in one of his numerous books, or remember it from

conversations he often had with groups of students. Wherever I heard this
piece of advice, it stuck. To those of us who were going into parish ministry,
Dr. Oates counseled, "Remember to take care of yourselves. The church isn't
good about taking care of its ministers. Most churches will accept everything
you want to give. If you go into the ministry looking for somebody else to
take care of you, you will likely be disappointed and wind up overworked,
angry, depressed, and out of touch with God, yourselves, and your family."

Dr. Oates wasn't being hypercritical of everyone in the church.
Obviously, any of us who have been pastors have met the overly demanding
member. For whatever reasons, this person expects us to be everything to
him or her, and both parties wind up frustrated. No matter how hard we
work, it is never enough. Fortunately, most people in the church are more
understanding. They recognize that ministry in the church is demanding.
Some may comment to the pastor that he or she is working hard, but most
people are reluctant to tell their ministers what they should or should not be
doing. Often, the assumption is that whatever time and energy we invest in
the life of the church is what we choose. People will accept whatever their
pastors give, and the majority of the congregation often knows little of the
breadth and intensity of our ministries.

The result is that as ministers we become depressed and angry while the
church people are confused about what is happening to their pastor. Then, as
the pastor becomes more emotionally debilitated and less effective in the per-
formance of ministry, the congregation becomes more negatively critical, and
the cycle of pain increases. While pastors are responsible for self-care, some
things about ministry today need to be taken into account. These factors
may contribute to our anxiety about our call and task as ministers and, therefore, need to be identified.

First, there isn't the appreciation for the vocation of ministry that once
was a part of our culture. Several years ago I sat next to an attractive, well-
dressed woman on an airplane flight from Richmond, Virginia, to Charlotte,
North Carolina. One of her daughters sat on the other side of her mother.
Her husband and two other children sat on the row in front of us. "We're
going to Disney World," she said. I didn't tell her where I was headed. My
destination wasn't nearly as exciting. Making polite conversation, the woman
asked me what I did for a living. In a moment of utter irrationality, I replied,
"I'm a seminary professor." Usually, I just say, "I'm a minister." How many
people really know what a seminary is? Besides, if you don't say seminary
crisply, it sounds like "cemetery." Professor—that's another frightening

image: some guy dressed in a tweed coat who wanders around the campus late in the afternoon trying to remember where he parked his bike.

Well, I'd already done the damage. "I'm a seminary professor." The woman looked perplexed. I didn't even want to try to explain my job. "My husband is a dentist," she responded. She didn't have to explain. I knew what dentists did. I also knew there was more money in cavities and crowns. I started to tell her that one day I'd have a crown because of my earthly sacrifice, but I decided I'd already caused enough confusion for the short stretch between Richmond and Charlotte.

Granted, I would have been better served if I had answered "minister." My impression was that the church didn't hold a central place in her family's life, but probably at some time she'd gone to church. At least, perhaps, she had watched ministers at baptisms, weddings, or funerals and had a vague sense that we were important at significant passages in people's lives. However, as I tried to "unpack" the vocation of seminary professor and explain that I really was a "minister," I had the sense that she viewed my calling as ill-defined and hardly worth the time to explain what I meant. "My husband is a dentist," the woman on her way to Disney World said. His calling was clear.

A second factor ministers encounter these days is the decreasing relevance of the church. While many churches are viable and strong, others struggle to maintain institutional footing. Instead of the primary energy of the congregation being spent to help the church minister to the world, the constant fretting over dwindling attendance, enthusiasm, and finances drains energy. We wonder: Why aren't we reaching more young people? Where are the young couples who will be our future leaders? What happened to the commitment of people in assuming places of responsibility in the church? The result of this kind of decline and questioning is a pervasive anxiety that breeds despair but also causes churches to search for the "latest" solutions to their problems.

For example, take the issue of "worship wars." I'm certainly not opposed to innovations in worship or in preaching. In fact, we need to examine honestly what we do, and effectiveness is a legitimate criterion. However, a minister's personality, gifts, and theology of worship will affect dramatically his/her ability to lead or to preach in certain contexts. While some ministers seem to have the ability to adapt to most situations, many ministers do not choose or feel highly uncomfortable in worship situations that aren't congenial to their gifts and their views of worship.

When churches are in difficulty, they tend to think pragmatically. What can we do to draw a crowd? What do we need to change in order to attract people? Pragmatism is not without its merits. There's nothing commendable about a church's declining when it has the advantages that should be attracting people. If a church is stodgy, rigid, and out of touch with people's needs, that church needs to make changes. Also, if a preaching minister speaks in ways that reflect no knowledge of changing communicative forms, then that minister needs to understand that one of the significant factors in any preaching event is the congregation—what they need to hear and how best to communicate to them.

With this said, however, we need to resist the idea that the only way to worship or the only way to communicate is through the style of the MTV generation. I have serious theological concerns. The form in which something is communicated does affect the substance. What we have in the Bible is largely a connected story in which the protagonist is God and where Jesus comes and moves into the flow of human history. We don't have episodic swatches of God here and there, now and then. We have a story of the relentless love of God, and the story culminates for us as Christians in the life, death, and resurrection of the anointed one. To say it another way, the church has a past, present, and future, and all of those need to be taken seriously.

A second concern I have relates to ecclesiology, the doctrine of the church. The New Testament seems to delight in the fact that in Christ so many disparate people and groups are brought together. This was a miracle in the first century, and as Paul so insightfully writes, "in Christ Jesus" this unity happens. This is the miracle. People who normally have no reason to come together are brought together by their love for the God who loves them. We need to be careful that in our desire to speak to certain generations, we not destroy the togetherness that for writers such as Luke and Paul was generated by a shared experience of God in Christ.

This makes the experience of preaching even more challenging. It requires preachers to evaluate their messages and to make certain that they are not preaching simply from who they are and what they've experienced. This means that in preparing a message the minister, figuratively speaking, takes into his study a wide variety of those to whom he will speak. While the minister certainly reads the biblical text through the lens of her or his own background and experience, that shouldn't be the only lens through which the text is viewed. Otherwise, the implied listener to every sermon is simply a projection of the minister.

This approach to ecclesiology also demands maturity on the part of church members. If we approach worship solely on the basis of what we want, we wind up with a self-centeredness antithetical to the whole purpose of the church. Certainly, we want preaching and worship that speaks to us, that is faithful to the biblical witness, and that is shared with us by leaders who care about what they do. However, we need to ask the theological question: When we gather as a community of faith, do we seek to praise and glorify God? Are we listening for a word from God even if it is a disturbing word for us, or do we want something just to make us feel better about ourselves? Perhaps even worse, are we looking simply to be entertained?

I'm becoming more convinced that there are many ways to do worship. However, very few ministers can lead every kind of worship service and preach faithfully in every kind of context. Additionally, some of the new forms of worship devalue the spoken word. One of the mantras of some of the new ways of worship is that the visual has replaced the verbal. The preached word is seen as out of step, especially with a younger generation accustomed to fast-moving images. Granted, this has placed new responsibility on those of us whose vocations revolve around crafting and conveying words. However, the assumption that the verbal has gone the way of the dinosaur conveys to preaching ministers and those considering the call to preach that preaching is irrelevant.

Several years ago my wife gave me a porcelain figure of a preacher. She thought it was cute and would look nice in my office. I tried to be grateful, but I was a little defensive. The porcelain figure depicted a minister who had eaten too much and who had exercised too little. His eyes were lifted to the heavens while his right index finger pointed at me as I held the figure. What bothered me most was the expression on his face. He looked out of it. His face reflected the stereotype that many people have of ministers. You might invite the pastor to give the blessing at your party, fix him a nice "doggy bag" filled with fried foods, and then send him home before the fun began.

I put the figure in my office. After all, it was a gift from Diane. But once in awhile, I still ask her, "Is that how you see me? Am I just a voice crying in the wilderness? Am I that out of touch with life?" Diane reassures me that I'm reading too much into the figure. "It's just a figure of a cute little minister." One of these days I need to tell my wife that I really don't want to be thought of as "a cute little minister."

What minister doesn't aspire to speak to all of the people all of the time? Maybe that's too lofty a goal. At least, however, we want to know that once in a while our words can slice across generations and genders. We need to believe that our words can touch those who sit in the front pews, whose faces we see, and those who sit in the far reaches of the balcony, too far away for us to see if they've been moved to laughter or to tears.

Preaching has been buried at other times in history only to rise from the dead. In our desire to make the church relevant, we need to be careful and thoughtful about simply mirroring communicative forms like MTV or fast-paced video games. We should ask what we can learn from these forms as preachers. Obviously, we need to recover the image-richness of Jesus' teaching and the power of his stories to convey life-changing truths. We need to recognize that God comes most clearly to us in the Incarnation. How do we now incarnate this Word so that the aliveness and activity of God are seen as present realities and not just as "once-upon-a-time" experiences? Yet, in our desire to be relevant and to reach people, we, as the church, should not forget the great truths of our faith. These truths involve someone's dying on a cross, and these truths call us to take up our own crosses. Discipleship isn't finding the easy way or the path of least resistance. Discipleship is demanding. Whatever ways a church chooses to communicate the faith, this call to radical obedience needs to be front and center. If not, we may draw a crowd, but what do we have if we gain the whole world and lose our souls in the process?

A third issue with which ministers deal isn't new, but I believe the difficulty is increasing. The pastor of almost any church is expected to perform multiple and diverse tasks. These often call for a different set of gifts and abilities. Frustration, anxiety, and anger abound when the pastor is unable or unwilling to set boundaries and limits and tries to be all things to all people. Feeding those feelings are the unreasonable expectations that some in the congregation have for the minister.

While I teach at the seminary, I often serve as interim pastor at nearby churches. One of the most intriguing things for me is to watch a church decide about the job description or expectations for its new pastor. Almost invariably, the number one desired attribute is good preaching skills. Sometimes, this is defined more specifically. A good preacher is someone whose sermons are biblically based, theologically insightful, and connected to the lives of the listeners. One church specified that it wanted a preaching minister who effectively combined "style and substance." Of course, the list of qualities wanted in a minister doesn't end with proclamation. Most churches want a skilled pastoral caregiver, someone who relates well to all groups in the church, a visionary who knows how to inspire and manage a team of other ministers as well as oversee the entire church operation. At the same time, this minister is expected to have a strong relationship with God that is evident in character and conduct. In addition, the minister is expected to serve as an example of a devoted spouse and parent.

Frankly, I've never met any minister who does all of these things equally well. I've met some who have tried to do all these things effectively, but most of them either recognized the impossibility and struck some accommodation within themselves, or they left the ministry in bitterness. As a pastor, I recall struggling with the multiplicity of roles I had to play. I wanted to please everyone. I wanted God to be pleased. I wanted the church to do well. Looking back, a lot of what I struggled with was internally generated. Because the pastorate involved so many facets, I found myself spinning from one task to the next, many times not seeing much connection among the things I was doing. Much of my self-image was built on how well I did. Unfortunately, what I often sacrificed is now what I see as most important—my relationship to God and time and focus for my own family. In retrospect, it's sad for me to see how long it took to begin to understand how skewed my priorities were.

While I recognize that much of my sadness was self-generated, I also believe the church contributes by its overexpectations of ministers. Most ministers are trained in theology, Bible, church history, spiritual formation, and ministry studies such as pastoral care and preaching. While some seminaries and divinity schools offer courses in leadership, administration, conflict resolution, and other management skills, most schools don't place their primary emphases in these areas. Those of us who teach in seminaries realize we only have a certain number of courses that we can reasonably expect students to take. We want our graduates to be well trained, but we are not a business school training executives. While our seminary, as other seminaries, wants our graduates to be effective leaders, we want to produce ministers who think theologically and who have the skills to help people interpret life in light of God's presence and power.

For me as a parish minister, this was always a dilemma. Where do I put the strongest investment of my time and energy? I identified the preaching/teaching task as my first responsibility. This meant that I needed sufficient time and concentration to pray and to think about the needs of the congregation, to plan a sermon schedule, to focus on the biblical text for that Sunday, to read, to decide what I wanted to say, and then to plan how I wanted to organize the sermon. Additionally, the sheer act of delivering the sermon required an enormous amount of physical and emotional energy. As a pastor, you want to have something to say. People have given you the gift of their time. They listen for the word from God through you, and some of those who listen are in desperate need of bread and water for the journey. A minister who takes seriously the call to preach needs to have her or his needs taken seriously by the congregation.

Perhaps both ministers and churches need to reevaluate their expectations of themselves and each other. As ministers, we need to lower our anxiety about pleasing everyone and doing every facet of our job equally well. We need to communicate honestly to churches about what we do well and what we don't do well. If a pastor search committee insists on everything being done well, let that congregation live with the consequences. The simple fact is that a church won't find that perfect combination of abilities, and if it believes it has, it will find out quickly that someone hasn't been telling the whole truth.

Churches need to be more realistic and more compassionate. As a minister in the church, I worked hard because I do love the church and believe deeply in its ministry. While I believe I was successful, I also saw what the stress of trying to be all things to all people was doing to me. I had trouble relaxing, sleeping, and focusing on the concerns of my family. I would work seven days a week, and even then felt I didn't have time to do the work and especially to prepare to preach as well as I would like. As I've said, much of that was self-generated. While I wanted to prove myself, I had and still have a love for the church of Jesus Christ. To me, the calling to be somebody's pastor is the highest call in the world. Intellectually, I understood I was a human being. I preached passionate sermons about being sustained and strengthened by the grace of God. What I had trouble doing was internalizing my own words. With this confession, I want to talk about some ways we may care for ourselves as pastors.

REMEMBER GOD'S CARE FOR US

Preaching in a church in South Carolina recently, I had a serendipitous experience. Instead of sitting in the pulpit area facing the congregation, the pastor said, "Let's sit on the front row for the first part of the service." As the prelude was played, I looked at the communion table in the front and saw those familiar words etched in the wood, "This do in remembrance of me." Jesus asked his disciples to continue to gather at the table and to remember him. Almost every church to which I go has a similar table with similar words. As a teenager, I was less than impressed with the times our church celebrated communion. It was usually at the end of what for me had already been a lengthy service. I listened to the minister lift the wafers and say, "This is my body." I even recollect sermons in which our pastor carefully pointed out what this meant in our faith tradition. "This isn't really the body. It represents the body." So through this symbol we remembered Jesus.

The problem is that I really had no understanding of what we were supposed to do. Were we supposed to think about miracles Jesus performed and see if we could recreate that moment in our minds? Were we supposed to remember Jesus' teachings and try to commit ourselves to deeper obedience? The word "memory" had little taste for me. The past was a place for people to hide. I would hear adults talk about the way things used to be. "Do you remember the Great Depression?" "Do you remember when Lindbergh crossed the Atlantic?" Jesus said, "This do in remembrance of me."

I saw the Table that night in South Carolina and thought, "Life really does change." Memory is vital to me. Often, I retrace the past remembering people, places, and events that have shaped me. But what does it mean to remember? I still remember my baptism. I recall the place, the pastor, and the people who began their spiritual journeys with me that night. The minister told us that in baptism we remembered who we were and whose we were. Those of us who were baptized died to our old selves and were raised to walk in newness of life. A part of that new life, as the minister reminded us, is that like Jesus at his baptism, we realized that our identity was being the beloved children of God.

How fresh that sense of who I really was seemed to me in the days following my baptism. God seemed so incredibly close—so eager to love me, to forgive me, to remind me that God's love for me was unconditional. What a breath of new air! I'd always viewed love for me as conditional. Love was the reward for achievements, for good behavior, or for not making mistakes. I would be loved if I did something perfect. In looking back, I don't think my parents meant to convey that message. In fact, I recall times that they loved me when I had done something wrong. But for whatever reasons, I had arrived at a stance toward life that saw love as highly conditional. How special it was for me at my baptism to be reminded that God was with me, for me, and by me no matter what I thought or did.

Yet, in the years after my baptism I lost touch with that intimate sense of God's presence. Some people might blame education. I went to college and seminary to prepare for my calling. Of course, I have negative criticisms of my education. I wish there had been more emphasis on my spiritual formation and the interior life of the minister. I wish I had learned not just an analytical approach to biblical texts but also how to enter them devotionally and reverently. Yet, I take responsibility for what happened. Nobody discouraged me from prayer. Nobody said a minister's personal communion with God wasn't essential to a life of service. What happened was that I left behind those things that had nourished and reminded me of whose I am, and I entered the ministry with the desire to get approval and acceptance from others.

That's why the words on the Lord's Supper Table meant so much: "This do in remembrance of me." Remembering is not living in the past. It's pulling into the present the deepest realities that have sustained us and will sustain us. Remembering is knowing that what made a difference can still make a difference. In many ways life seems infinitely more complicated and complex than when I first began to see that God loves me simply for who I am. I am a husband and a father. I have been a pastor. I have taught preaching. I have been in the church and understand better what its demands can do to me and others. I know myself better. I know how susceptible I am to the desire to please and have others like me. I understand how those things can replace any sense that God is with me. I fall victim easily to the presumption that I have to make something happen for God rather than prayerfully discerning where God is at work and joining God in those places. Even as a minister, I can become oblivious to the sacred, especially in the ordinary things of life. I see the surface but not the depths. I see the wind and the waves but not the one who says, "Peace." I'm afraid of what others may think. I'm afraid I will fail and therefore, in my mind, will be no good.

This is why it's important for me to remember that even in my fears and anxieties, God loves me unconditionally. This awareness can make all the difference in my preaching. When I preach from fear and anxiety, I'm distant from God, others, and myself. I end up trying to manipulate some kind of response from people that makes me feel better about myself. That takes enormous energy and invariably fails. However, when I preach knowing I'm loved by the Gracious Other and that those who listen are also loved, I can come to the pulpit with the awareness that God is already there, and I join with what God is making happen.

ACCEPT OURSELVES
AS A GIFT FROM GOD

In the New Testament, one of the most fascinating Greek words is *charis*. When this word refers to God, it's usually translated "grace." However, when *charis* applies to humankind, it is most often rendered "gratitude." As Fred Craddock has said on numerous occasions, "The final work of Grace is to make us gracious." You and I have met gracious people in our lives. These people have a remarkable way of moving outside the stream of their own needs and giving care to us. We don't know the stories of all these people. We know they must have experienced life much as we have. Undoubtedly, they have had their disappointments. Yet something has "tenderized" them. These people seem to be at peace with who they are, and they have the capacity to give their love and encouragement to others.

It seems to me that all of ministry including preaching is connected intimately to our self-image. Am I worthy? Do I accept gratefully what God has made me? Or do I spend too much of my time trying to get from others a sense of my own worth?

For those of us who are ministers, it's sometimes hard to name our motivations. My motivations have been a mixture of things. There is a part of me that I would like you to know. I do care about people. I like to think that for the most part I'm kind and considerate. When I was a pastor and now as a professor, I believe people felt and feel comfortable sharing things with me and know that I empathize with them. I'm faithful to my commitments. For thirty-four years I've been married to Diane and have loved her and my two children. I've tried to be a faithful minister. In the best way I know how, I've attempted to follow God's purpose and have tried to be a person of integrity and responsibility. This is the part of me that I would like you to know.

But there are other currents in my life. It's been hard for me to identify and name this other side of who I am. I struggle with low self-esteem. At times, this led me to be jealous of other ministers and their successes. I've viewed many of my fellow ministers as competitors and not as colleagues. Additionally, I've often seen my preaching as a means to be affirmed by others. Instead of approaching the pulpit as a place to give something, I have come to the pulpit to get appreciation, respect, and love. Almost unconsciously, I've seen the preaching event as the place where I perform, and the response of the people is my applause.

I see how much anxiety and stress this has placed on me. Preaching done from the best motivations is a fatiguing experience. We put so much of ourselves into the birth, the exegesis, the organization, and the delivery of a message. All the time, we prayerfully ask God to direct our efforts. However, the more we see preaching as a way to get our need for love met, the more exhausting it becomes. We're always thinking about how the listeners respond to us. How can I be clever? How can I be cute? How can I be creative? Instead of our message being a gift we give without any thought of return, it becomes only a gift to get others to give us the affirmation we want.

One of the significant mystical traditions of the church has been labeled "apophetic." Apophetic prayer is the emptying of ourselves, of thoughts, of compelling images, so that we are brought to the position of simply "being before God." In apophetic prayer, we try to put aside our "doing." We attempt to empty ourselves of achievements and failures, of those things that in our "doing" kind of culture have shaped our self-image. What we hopefully discover is that our being, our core self, is the creation of a God who loves us and who has pronounced us as very good.

For me, the discovery of the potency of this kind of prayer has been a journey—and not always an even journey. I have allowed myself to be encrusted with all the barnacles of doing so that it's difficult to chip those away and to be empty before God. More than that, my whole approach to life has been based on conditional love. I have usually found it hard to believe that anybody would love me if that person knew my fears, my anxiety, my resentments, and my depression. For me, apophetic prayer is so alien to the way I have done life. Yet, desperation drives us to seek new paths. I am tired of approaching preaching as a way to get approval. Whatever approval I may get, it never seems enough.

What if you and I could approach the preaching event as the giving of our gifts first to God and then to others? What if the sermon was more like an offering than a public presentation, a gift in which the tangible response of our listeners wasn't the gauge by which we measured our success or failure?

What would that do to our preaching, and what would that mean for us as proclaimers? That doesn't mean we don't work at ways to refine and communicate the message. It does lessen the anxiety about how we're doing and how we're being received. As Søren Kierkegaard reminded us, it places God as the primary listener, and our deepest desire is to give God the gift of our love. God understands the pressures that we ministers face. God understands that there are times when exhaustion and concern about meeting the needs of our congregation leave us with little energy and focus when we enter the pulpit. Yet, God loves us unconditionally. God knows that we ministers often over-expect what we can do. This gracious God loves us tenderly and simply accepts the gift we can give.

LEARN TO REPLENISH OURSELVES

Let's admit it. Some ministers are lazy. Some ministers lack the motivation to structure their lives even in a minimal way and thus spend countless, wasted hours trying to get started. I'm really not writing for these ministers. Laziness in a minister is difficult to tolerate. The call to minister is far too important. If a pastor has trouble managing time, then that pastor needs to get help to learn how best to use the time he or she has. Much of ministry is unsupervised. We have tasks to perform, but nobody gives us a schedule to follow. Additionally, unexpected events arise in the life of the parish. Somebody dies, and the pastor is expected to visit the family, plan the funeral service, and speak words that eulogize the deceased and comfort the family. A vital early lesson for ministers involves determining their best times to do certain tasks. For example, I learned that the most creative time for me is in the morning. I scheduled my sermon planning for the hours when I was more awake and alert. I let church members know my study hours. I could be interrupted in an emergency, but only in an emergency. This was no time for someone to call to say, "My friends and I were wondering where that verse was about 'lilies of the fields.'" That can wait!

When I talk about the need to replenish ourselves, I'm usually speaking to ministers who take their ministry seriously and who are conscientious, probably too conscientious, about doing well in every aspect of ministry. The fact is that as a church, we face a major problem in our day.

First, many of our best young people are not choosing the ministry and especially the pastorate as a vocation. This is supported by numerous studies.

Why? Answers vary. The ministry has lost some of its stature in recent years. Second, numerous denominations are embroiled in controversy, and that's hardly inviting to individuals who want to be involved in something positive and not spend all of their time in ecclesiastical wars. Third, the responsibilities of the pastor have escalated. Bright young people see that churches function much like a business, and the pastor is the C.E.O. If somebody wants to be the head of a company, why not go to business school and make considerably more money? Finally, for the sake of this discussion, aspiring young ministers see some older ministers who have grown cynical, angry, and deeply discouraged about their work as a pastor. Some of these veterans have opted out of the pastorate, while others continue their ministries with little or no enthusiasm for what they do.

These things deeply concern me and should concern everyone who loves the church. Truthfully, some people should not have gone into the ministry in the first place. I know this seems counter to the idea of God's call. However, the home churches of young people headed to seminary or divinity school need to be more discerning and more honest in their counsel. The pastorate demands both a set of gifts and a set of skills. Those of us who teach young ministers try to help them with what they need to know and to refine their gifts. However, a student with serious interpersonal problems will have great difficulty as a minister. As people who care for churches and for these young students, we simply need to do a better job of describing what is needed in specific ministry positions and helping guide the person to a vocation where he or she can be fulfilled, not frustrated.

At the same time, both ministers and churches need to work together to recover the image of the pastor as a spiritual companion. We need to work to encourage the life of prayer and study for ministers as well as for the rest of the congregation. The idea that any pastor can keep feeding listeners spiritually while not taking time to renew his or her spirit is fallacious. Churches will suffer because the preaching and teaching ministry of the pastor will become more and more shallow. It's simply impossible to meet with committees, motivate congregations to meet budgets, encourage laypeople to discharge responsibilities they have assumed, and at the same time tend faithfully to the needs of the minister's spirit.

Because I teach preaching, I'm expected to say this. The fact is that I teach preaching because I believe this. What I believe is that the first and foremost calling of any pastor is to be as effective and as nurturing as possible. The pulpit is the place where we will have contact with the most people in almost every week. Most of the folks give us the gift of their attention. In my opinion, public worship and proclamation are the center of a congregation's life. The worship service is the hub from which the spokes of all the ministries radiate. How tragic it is when a pastor gathers up the broken pieces of a few words and illustrations on Saturday night and then enters the church house on Sunday to feed hungry people. Some churches need to reexamine what they expect of a pastor and make sure they encourage the minister to have adequate time to pray, to prepare, and to preach.

At the same time, ministers need to take responsibility to make the time to nourish their inner life and to prepare themselves for the high hour of public worship and proclamation. Unfortunately, some ministers really don't like the work of preparation. Gregarious pastors feed off the interaction they have with people but sometimes neglect the times when they need to move to the place of study. All of us as ministers should recognize the kinds of people we are and then work on areas that may not be our strengths. While some ministers may neglect the study, others spend all their time doing word studies, looking at commentaries, or trying to find one key insight on which the sermon will turn. Usually, these ministers bring sermons heavy with historical background and thick with the nuances of Hebrew or Greek words—information that is exciting to the minister. The problem is that the pastor spends so much time in the study that little time remains to prepare the sermon for the sanctuary. The sermon resembles a term paper citing one theologian after another, but the message the pastor speaks never gets internalized in his or her life and lacks connection to the lives of the listeners.

But my primary concern is for ministers who spend too little time prayerfully engaging the Bible and whose Sunday sermons are meandering efforts in search of some point. The sermon is pointless. The message may be a jumble of internet stories, a few thoughts about the biblical text that have no relationship to each other, or whatever ideas we can glean from the Bible as we sneak peeks at the text while the rest of the church sings its faith in hymns. Even worse is the sermon that begins with the reading of a biblical text, when the rest of the message has nothing to say about the biblical word for the day.

Is there a simple remedy for the lack of prayerful study and preparation? Can we study and enjoy it? Is there a sermon shortcut? Some of us may have tried to find a shortcut when we were in college. We read the "Cliff Notes" but found that wasn't enough for the test, and we never really got the flavor of the book. Now, ministers can get "microwaveable" sermons on the internet. Just download them, warm them up, and we have a message. Except this approach to preparation misses two essential experiences.

First, there is a good word to be said for discipline. I know "discipline" doesn't sound appealing, but it is necessary to the well-rounded life of a minister. Even with interruptions that may come, we want to have a schedule for each week that includes adequate time for study, organization, and preparing ourselves for the delivery of the message. We want to have a pattern for how we do this preparation. Within that system, we want to allow sufficient time for study, for deciding what we want to say, and for planning how we want to structure the movement of the sermon. Then we, as preaching ministers, want to sit in front of our message so that we hear it well and are engaged by it in the deepest places of our being. When we speak the words, we want to experience with the congregation the power of the God who has moved with us through all the prayer and preparation in which we've been engaged. Discipline is a way in which those of us who minister to others can care for ourselves by taking the time we need to pray and study.

A second reason for us to develop the discipline of study is that we get to hear the biblical words for ourselves. Nobody hears the text for Sunday more than the preacher. When I prayerfully read the words from which I'm going to preach, I'm often the one who is touched. When I approach the Bible not just analytically but also devotionally, I receive a word for my own journey. No minister is exempt from being human. Most of us who enter ministry are sensitive people. We try to develop appropriate distance from church members so that we don't get sick with everybody who goes to the hospital. We want to have enough distance so that we can minister. But most of us feel life as well as think life, and as we enter our studies, who knows how God may speak? As the Benedictine monks have reminded us with their concept of "lectio divina," we "chew" on the words of the Bible and read with an openness that lets the words invade our own lives.

We are not trying "to get up a sermon." We're discovering a message that hopefully becomes both our message and the congregation's message. As preachers, we both hear what we say and say what we hear.

LEARN TO BE SOME THINGS
TO SOME PEOPLE

It's impossible to characterize all ministers as having the same personalities and needs. Ministers are different. They are different in temperament, in gifts, in relational skills, in the ability to handle stressful situations, and in almost every other dimension of human experience. However, studies done of ministers show that many of us have a high need to please people. This is certainly true of me. When I went into the ministry, I had the illusion that I was going to be all things to all people. Intellectually, I have found through the years that this is impossible. However, as with so many other parts of our lives, my emotional response has not caught up with what I know in my head. Therefore, I'm still brittle when I'm negatively criticized about areas of my ministry. That's particularly true when I'm negatively critiqued aloud about my preaching. For me, that's the core of my identity as a minister.

Each year I ask my introductory preaching class to listen to me in a seminary chapel service and then write a two-page critique of the message. Since the class involves my assessing their preaching and giving them feedback, I want the students to understand that all of us, including their teacher, can grow in our communicative skills.

All of that sounds noble. However, when the day comes for me to preach and for them to evaluate me, I'm not sure this process is a good idea. My students take this too seriously. I've learned not to ask students for feedback unless I'm ready for it. The students say affirming things, but then the other shoe drops. They start saying things like, "You told us to have a clear point in the sermon, but you tried to say too many things. You said we should be clear in our connections and transitions in our sermons, but I don't know how you got from here to there." I could go on, but you get the point. I want to hear the students' criticisms, but I don't want to hear them! At about the tenth paper, I start to say, "They're just students. What do they know?" But, of course, they do know what moves them, what persuades them, what causes them to think more deeply about God and about life, and they know what helps and what hinders those things.

I often think about my times as a pastor and reflect on the ministries of pastors I know. For the most part, people in churches understand the multiplicity of ministerial tasks and are accepting of less than perfection from their ministers. Some folks are generous in their praise and let us know that what we're doing makes a difference. However, pastors know that churches do have people who are negative or seemingly indifferent to what we do. We learn that even our most valiant efforts in ministry don't please some people, and we also learn that some in the congregation never give us feedback. We simply don't know, for example, whether our preaching has any impact on their lives.

What do we do as ministers? For one thing, we reexamine the priority we put on positive feedback. This has been a lifelong issue for me. Positive feedback has been far too important. I approached preaching as a place where I was on display, and then I waited at the back door for comments like, "What a wonderful sermon." When somebody made no comment about the sermon, I assumed she didn't like it. Outgoing people, shy people, people for whom kind words came easily, people who probably never even told their children and spouses that they loved them—it made no difference. I was an equal opportunity seeker of praise and felt hurt and rejected when someone didn't say the sermon was "really good," or even better, "great."

Part of reexamining the priority we put on praise is to re-image the preaching event. Is it a public exhibit of our abilities where we display what we've found in the biblical text that nobody in the history of the church has ever seen? Is preaching the place where we dazzle the congregation with our rhetorical skills? If so, then we will seek the instant gratification of listeners who let us know that we have "wowed" them. We also will be discouraged by those who don't respond with the affirmation we seek. What if we saw proclamation, however, in a different way? We give the gift we have that day. Obviously, we want to give a good gift. But we as the givers are not the primary focus. It's giving the gift of ourselves and our words and then trusting God to use them as God's Spirit does the deep work of changing people's lives. When I speak with the intention of shaping the outcome, I get into trouble. Instead of feeding the listeners, I usually want them to feed me. When I preach from the position of "I'm not O.K.," then I view the congregation largely as people who are there to meet my needs.

In addition to reexamining the premium we ministers sometimes put on positive feedback, we also have to learn to accept being "some things to some people." My son David and I share an affinity for "shaved ices." During the summer, we have a favorite place to go to get them. In case you haven't had one, you've missed a treat. It's shaved ice with flavor on the top. Most people like a single flavor like cherry or vanilla. The place David and I go, however, combines flavors with wonderful names for their combinations. The store has "Romantic Rhapsody." It's 1/3 cherry, 1/3 vanilla, and 1/3 coconut.

Don't ask me what any of those flavors have to do with romance or rhapsody. However, David and I decided we wanted to get all the flavors by the end of the summer, so we order these strange combinations because we can get three instead of one. Our goal is to taste every flavor even though that means we'll only get a fraction of each one.

One my frustrations as a pastor is that I really never savored the flavor of any one thing I did, and my ministry sometimes seemed fragmented—filled with bits and pieces. It's tempting to blame this on church members who asked me to do a variety of things. However, in retrospect, I recognize I was the one saying "yes," and much of that was motivated by my desire to please and to be liked. While preaching was my first love as a pastor, I never said to people, "This is the heart of my identity vocationally. Preaching is what I see as my essential task, and for me to preach and teach effectively, I will need space, time, and focus to do this in a way that satisfies us all."

It takes courage to do this. Basically, we are saying to the church, "I can't do everything you may expect. I have some priorities as a minister. One of these is to have something meaningful to say when I stand to preach." Contrary to some impressions, our seminary education isn't the end of the input we need. We don't live out of that education exclusively all the days and nights of our ministry. Preaching is hard work. It takes discipline. It takes time. It takes energy. Most pastors know the empty feeling on Monday mornings. Something has gone out of us, and we have to reenergize spiritually, emotionally, and physically.

Sometimes, I look at the ministerial ordination certificate in my office. How grateful I am for the trust of a church in me. How appreciative I am for other congregations that have let me be their pastor. I so wanted to fulfill their expectations and not disappoint them. However, I sometimes forgot about my own needs, the needs of my family, and frankly, I forgot about my inability to do it all. Even the ordination certificate doesn't remove me from the frailties of my own humanity. I can do some things. I can't do other things. What is the minister doing in this confession? He or she is simply saying, "I'm human."

What Is Pastoral Preaching?

When I was thinking about the order of subjects for a book like this, I deliberately began with a personal word and then tried to speak to the issue of a minister's self-care. It may seem odd to talk about these things before addressing the issue of pastoral preaching itself. Again, my deep conviction is that in the proclamation of the church, the messenger and the message can't be separated. Without care for ourselves as ministers and without attention to our spiritual formation, we risk anger, depression, inner emptiness, and any number of attitudes that affect both what we preach and the way we preach. Few images are sadder than the minister who has lost heart for what he or she is doing and who's simply trying to endure until retirement. The ministry is demanding. It takes its toll. Preaching takes a certain passion. Passion requires concentration and energy. Passion means that the pastor believes what she or he says can be the means for God to make a profound difference in the lives of listeners. When we do what we do and say what we say with little or no sense of the indwelling presence of God, we find ourselves running on momentum that has somewhere lost its meaning.

Yet, the preacher doesn't remain alone in trying to stay alive to the source of all words. There comes the time to go public. The pastor moves to the church house, the sanctuary, the fellowship hall, wherever the people have gathered, and now the moment has come to preach.

WHAT IS PREACHING?

What is preaching? I know those of us as proclaimers function with some ideas of what we're doing. What is that grand idea that guides us to the pulpit? Perhaps the most famous definition of preaching came from Phillips Brooks, rector of Trinity Church in Boston, Massachusetts, and chaplain at Harvard. Brooks said simply, "Preaching is truth through personality." That grand idea guided preaching that has affected so many lives.

Rather than a definition, I'd prefer to offer a description. All definitions, and all descriptions, fall far short of embracing everything that preaching can be, but it's more helpful to me to think about descriptive phrases that speak about aspects of preaching. Again, I want to begin by talking about the preaching event itself and then move to the issue of "pastoral preaching."

The Transcendence of Preaching

Some ministers today talk more about the "preaching event" than they do about "preaching." This may seem a small distinction to some people. However, the more organic phrase, "preaching event," captures the hope that something life-changing takes place in an activity that on the surface looks like one person speaking to people who may or may not be listening. The hope is that in the human words, the Divine Word is both heard and experienced. For this to happen, it's not enough to describe preaching in the traditional communicative pattern of speaker-message-listeners. Obviously, these elements are critical in communication. Some of us have had classes in public speech where professors exhorted us to speak from our diaphragms, to make eye contact with listeners, and to shape a speech that clearly and cogently presents a message people want or need to hear. We were taught the human dynamics of the speech process.

Preaching moves one great step beyond. While affirming what we learn about effective speaking, preaching makes the extraordinary claim that God is at work in our words and that people's lives can be fundamentally changed. Preaching can be a transformative experience. The essential difference isn't the innate gifts of the speaker or even the learned factors that make communication more attractive to the listener. Rather, in a mysterious, inexplicable way, the Word from God fills the words of women and men so that the possibility in preaching is that *God will happen in all of our lives.* Preaching is more than the verbal sequencing of words. It is an event where we prayerfully offer our words to God and allow the Word beyond all words to change us in the deepest places of our lives.

Recently, I preached a series of renewal services in Roanoke, Virginia. Some people in the church let me stay in their condominium. I awoke each morning, opened the blinds, and saw the majestic mountains that surround the Roanoke Valley. It was the beginning of October, and some of the trees were splashed in the beautiful colors of the season. One morning as I looked at the mountains I thought how different the scene was from what I knew as a boy. Growing up in Miami, Florida, we didn't have mountains. We had lots of water but no beautiful mountains with trees whose leaves turned extraordinary shades of red and yellow.

What we did have in Miami was a rise in one of the roads. Some people called it a hill, but that was a generous description. Sometimes our family would drive on a Sunday afternoon, park the car, and behold the rise in the road. We weren't the only ones. Other folks from the area would come to look at our "hill." I know this sounds strange. I guess we were all desperate for different scenery from the flat terrain of south Florida. Regardless, there we were on Sunday afternoons joining the other "flatlanders" to watch from different angles our "Miami mountain."

One summer we took a family vacation to western North Carolina. Can you imagine my surprise when I saw real mountains? That was an event! Somehow, my hometown hill was never the same. But suppose all I ever saw in my life was Miami. Ask me about mountains, and I would have told you about something very small. When I speak about the transcendent dimension of preaching, about God at work in our words, I feel as if I'm trying to describe something majestic but also something that reaches beyond my view and my comprehension. It's like the mountains I'd never seen. I'm tempted to talk about the small rises of the Spirit because that's often my view. As a pastor, I wonder how many times I have walked into the pulpit with little if any anticipation of Divine disclosure. How many times did I really expect anybody's life to be transformed? I had worked hard on the words of the sermon. But what about the Word? Perhaps I was tired, sometimes cynical, discouraged, angry, whatever! I wish that I had understood better that regardless of how I felt, I wasn't there to make God happen. God wanted to happen! That is God's nature. At the condominium where I stayed, I opened the blinds each morning. Isn't it interesting? No matter how I felt, the mountains were always there.

The Call to Give Our Best

To speak about preaching's transcendent dimension is not to diminish the importance of the person who preaches. Life-changing decisions in the lives of listeners are certainly effected through the Spirit of God. However, the

Holy One chooses people like you and me to speak words that we pray will be one of the ways transcendence is revealed.

Some people have referred to this as "incarnational preaching." This pattern does seem to explicate the way God works in the Bible and the way we sometimes have seen the Gracious Other touching our lives. To read the Bible is to conclude that God either has a strange sense of humor or that God makes bad choices when it comes to people. Look at the litany of heroes and heroines of the Bible. I know we have turned King David into a superhero, but after all, he did some things that would have gotten him fired from almost any church and probably arrested by the civil authorities. Let's call Uriah as a character witness for David: "Uriah, tell us about David's relationship with Bathsheba, your wife, and now that you know from reading the Bible, what do you think about being sent to front line of war where you were conveniently killed?"

Look at the first chapter of Matthew. This is Jesus' human genealogy. Not only can I not pronounce some of their names, but I also have no idea what contributions some made to the betterment of humankind. Several women are mentioned. People have taken great satisfaction that finally in a biblical genealogy, women are acknowledged. But who are some of these women? Let's put it mildly. They come with some baggage. If they were our children, we wouldn't want our neighbors to know what they did for a living. Yet, God found goodness in each of these people, and like us with our own families, they became active players in God's great salvation drama.

The pastoral minister has a unique role in that she or he lives among the parishioners. People in the congregation see us in the grocery store, at our children's Little League games, and in a variety of functions at the church. They know us between Sundays, and, therefore, our preaching is an extension of many ways in which we interact. Obviously, this can be an asset to our proclamation. If we are respected and seen as caring and warm individuals, people will bring that image of us when they listen. If people know that we can laugh and even have fun, they will see us as fellow human beings. It will also help to dispel the notion that the chief calling of ministers is to make other people miserable.

In our connection with people, those of us who are ministers need to keep in mind that one of the amazing things about God is that God molds and shapes the marred clay of our lives. Ministers live in the tension of expectations, both our own and other people's, and our humanity. Learning to live creatively with that tension is one of the factors in effective ministry.

For example, ministers do serve as models of caring and loving behavior. It's foolish for us to believe that what we do, what we say, and how we interact with other people aren't viewed in a different way than the actions of those who are not ministers. We become examples to others, and what I do and how I react to situations in life affect my credibility as a preacher. This is why it's imperative for us as ministers to know ourselves as well as possible and to be aware of our most vulnerable areas. Sometimes, our caring as ministers can lead to inappropriate relationships. Our desire for intimacy and love can blur appropriate boundaries between ourselves and someone for whom we may have tender feelings. Often, our desire to please others or to get people to respond in ways that we want can make us say things that reflect inappropriate anger or a sense of despair.

I remember a sermon I preached one Sunday that was loaded with anger toward the congregation. A part of me thought I was biblically prophetic. However, what emerged that Sunday was sheer hostility because I thought the people in the congregation weren't being committed at the level I expected. Rather than communicating a message, I turned the sermon into a catharsis for my anger. Fortunately, I had been at the church long enough that the people responded with care for me. I found again how many really good people are in the church. They wanted to know if I was tired, if I needed time away, or if there was something happening in the church with which they could help me. My sermon had no grace. However, the church couldn't have been more gracious.

As with many things we do or say, I've tried to analyze what was happening. I wish I had been more thoughtful before I preached the sermon, but as with so many things, the insight came after the incident. I shared this experience of preaching with a friend. "I was mad," I said. His response was interesting. "What I hear from you, Chuck, isn't madness but sadness." He said,

> It's a moment of sadness when we realize our limits as ministers—when we understand that no matter how hard we try or how persuasively we believe we preach, not everyone will respond the way we want. We also begin to realize our resistance to change as ministers. We all know better than we do. Sometimes our anger is really directed at ourselves as preachers as well as the listeners. When we overexpect of ourselves and others, we slip into despair and that painful awareness that we as ministers are not going to be able to bring in the reign of God as we once thought. At most, we will

change some things about ourselves and some things about others, but the really profound changes will be made by the Spirit of God.

My friend's words helped me gain a new perspective of a vulnerable part of me. When people don't respond to the message in the way I expect, they create a process in me that takes it very personally and sees it as a rejection of me. Some of us who choose ministry as a vocation want to be in control. The problem is that we deal with people who are free to say yes or no or to be indifferent. We don't control the ways of God or the ways of people. As Jesus reminded Nicodemus in the garden, the wind blows, and we don't know its origin or destiny.

This need to make things happen in the way we want directly affects our preaching. We see proclamation as an exceedingly personal enterprise. When people don't respond as we want or they don't change as quickly as we believe they should, we perceive the congregation as not liking us, what we say, or the way we say it. Instead of words among friends, preaching is seen as "us against them." Whether we realize it or not, the sadness, the anger, and the despair we feel as preachers slip into our words and our visual expressions. Instead of loving people into the presence of God, we marshal the forces of our words and attempt to coerce people in the direction we desire.

One of the most helpful things to me has been a renewed listening to my own sermons, especially those designed to change the attitudes or actions of people. As a minister prepares, he listens to the text and then to the words he will speak. A minister prepares the message, and she goes over in her mind and heart what she will say. When you and I think about it, we ministers actually listen to our sermons far more than the congregation listen to them. What I've found about myself is that I often resist the very things I want other people to accept. It's as hard for me to change as it is for most people to change. I get into patterns, and even when I know that I should change, it's incredibly difficult. Sometimes God breaks through, and I appropriate some truth for my life. Something changes, and I'm better for it. But like most people, I can hang on to the old ways, the old resentments, and the old sins even when I say I want to change.

What I hope is that this has infused my preaching with more empathy and deeper understanding. Certainly, I don't want to shy away from the call to be different and to reflect more in our lives the presence of Christ. Yet, I want to be kinder to myself and to others and to know that both preacher and hearers are pilgrims on a journey of growth that never ends.

When I talk about the character of the preacher and our being called to be the best of who we are, I want to speak about qualities like authenticity, humility, and vulnerability. The ministry is a place where some people have gone to try to hide from themselves. Voices change; faces take on more pious expressions; we fear our own humanity—and in the process we get out of touch with our feelings. We wear masks pretending that we feel no pain, and nothing or nobody can hurt us. We lose our souls and lose the gift of who we are and the individuals God has made us. We can't give ourselves in preaching because the sad truth is that somewhere, sometime, we lost ourselves.

The Need to Take Our Listeners Seriously

The physical arrangement of most places of worship communicates at least an implicit, if not an explicit, understanding of preaching. In reality, the preacher comes from the church. He or she shares a sense of humanity with others who are a part of the church. The person called to preach attends seminary or divinity school to receive an education that helps him or her prepare to care for souls. When that minister comes to preach, the distance between pulpit and pew is emphasized in the physical arrangement of sanctuary furniture. The pastor stands and faces the seated parishioners. Often, a large podium hides a significant portion of the minister's physical presence. If the pastor relies heavily on a manuscript or notes, his or her eyes are fixed on papers that lie on top of the podium, thus giving the furniture even more prominence. In addition, the pulpit is usually elevated. Here's the picture—preacher standing, preacher standing above, preacher standing above partially hidden behind the podium, while the congregation sits, with heads tilted up, listening to the words spilling down.

I've been a pastor long enough to know that while there are some communicative concerns with this arrangement, many people in the church have grown accustomed to it. There's comfort in the way we do things. When we as preachers alter the space in any way, we need to be intentional about what we're doing and to understand that many people consider familiarity a friend.

What guides us, though, in the preparation and the proclaiming of any message is the desire to have it heard by the listeners. Oral communication is designed to be heard. Within the "physical givens" of any situation, we want to do certain things that will help listeners hear our message. Primary among these is the preacher's respect for those who listen. This is especially challenging for a pastoral minister. As a pastor, we get to know some people at a fairly intimate level. These people also get to know us. We experience each other's strengths. We walk through difficult moments of life and discover in each other kindness, tenderness, and compassion. Sometimes we are amazed at the ability of people who encounter unexpected storms and respond in ways that give witness to God's sustaining mercy. As pastors, we have those who affirm our ministries and who seem to know just what to say or just what to do to encourage us.

We also have listeners whom we find more difficult to love. Some of these may be people who genuinely want to help us be better ministers. Their criticisms, while not always easy to receive, originate from a genuine concern for the welfare of the church and for our own well-being. Those of us who are ministers need to be more careful not to label as enemies those who express disagreement with us or who kindly suggest concerns that may make our ministry more effective. Dealing with negative criticism is difficult. We tend to personalize everything, and we often feel that a negative word about any part of our ministry condemns all that we are as a minister.

There is another form of negativity, however, with which ministers have to deal. Many churches have unhealthy people who make the pastor their target. This situation is exacerbated when the criticism meets an already tender part of us. Such negativity may take a variety of forms. It may be a control issue. Some churches have their "power brokers." These folks are used to controlling the decisions and the direction of the church. Suppose the pastor also has a high need for control. The result is a collision of wills. The one with the most power and votes wins. That's why a minister with the need for control must be wise in the timing of dealing with certain issues. It's not a sign of weakness to wait for the right time or even to accept that in this context, I will never be able to change this.

The issue may be theological. Divisions over doctrine or social issues trouble most denominations today. Problems arise when a person selects one or two issues and feels that the integrity of faith rests on the right response to those concerns. Of course, the right response is what that particular person has framed as the answer. That's the difficulty. Unless you and I as the ministers are prepared to give the "right" answer, we open ourselves to more accusations of our theology not being correct.

While there's certainly not an easy way for a pastor to deal with a church member who has focused the Christian faith on what we believe about the Bible or about stem-cell research, there are certain things we can do. Obviously, we have to be true to our own beliefs. However, we can reframe the question to fit a larger picture. For example, in my denomination, the words "inerrancy" and "infallibility" have been used to divide people into "conservatives" and "moderates." These words apply to how a person views biblical inspiration. One of the difficulties has been the "coded" way in which words like "inerrancy" and "infallibility" are sometimes used. "I believe the Bible is the inerrant word of God," a minister proclaims. What does that mean? In many ways, the word "inerrant" is both coded and divisive. It becomes a way of saying that I really believe the Bible, and those who don't use my adjectives are questionable in their beliefs about the Bible.

As ministers, we can reframe the question. The goal isn't to satisfy the other person; we can seldom do that unless we echo their words and exude their fervency. However, we can talk about our belief in the truths of the Bible and how through the inspired word of Scripture we are led to know God. It is important to express our points of view with confidence. This is not a formal debate or argument. Nobody is going to "win." We must state positively our convictions and not let anyone intimidate us with words or ideas we may not share. If that person wants to accuse us of not believing the right things, that's his or her issue. As pastors, we have far more urgent tasks than to try to appease someone we will never satisfy, and we don't want to let that individual make us angry or make us feel that our convictions are less meaningful than his or hers.

In 1983, our son David was diagnosed with a malignant brain tumor. Our family has moved through the valley. While David is still alive, my wife, daughter, and I have watched him become ravaged by the disease, the surgeries, and the radiation treatments. In the process, David has taught me more about trust in God and has exemplified an incredible faith. Ask me about the Bible, and I will tell you words that have sustained my family and me. Ask me if I believe the Bible is inerrant, and I will respond with the good news of a God who is faithful. Ask me if I believe the Bible is infallible, and I will tell about this God in Jesus Christ who gives strength for the journey. If you continue to ask me to use your words, I will respect you, but I will respect myself enough to respond in ways that express my faith.

When we preach about these matters, it's important to be respectful of ourselves and our hearers. It doesn't serve us well to "put down" people with different ideas or to imply that they are unenlightened. I don't respond well when somebody uses these abrasive tactics on me. I become defensive and more entrenched. Most of our beliefs serve the purpose of stabilizing us in a confusing, changing world. As Seward Hiltner pointed out, we live with "dated emotions" or "dated beliefs." At some point, we grasp hold of the rock so the flood won't sweep us away. Perhaps the flood has passed, and it's time for some of us to let go of the rock and move on in our lives.

A good preacher realizes that she or he has also grasped some rocks, and knows to let go of certain emotions or ideas in order to hold on to something more reasonable and life-giving. This preacher doesn't condemn the congregation because some people aren't as enlightened. This preacher doesn't bash other people's notions and make them feel foolish and benighted. Rather, in a kind, confident way, this preacher shares the faith that guides his or her life, respecting the hearers enough to allow them a personal response to that faith, whether it be yes or no.

An interesting phenomenon in our time is the increased radicalizing of the world's faiths. As I write this, our own nation lives in the sad aftermath of thousands of people killed, apparently at the impulse of a group of people who use the name of God to justify destruction. While most Christians probably wouldn't think about physically killing someone else, we do inflict wounds on each other with our harsh rhetoric and the questioning of someone else's faith because that person doesn't use all the words in our religious vocabulary. Even the forms of our most central focus—public worship—have divided churches and caused people to write about "worship wars."

How does a minister speak in this kind of environment? Somehow we need to avoid the siege mentality and try to continue to speak hopeful, care-filled words to the lives of people. We don't know how people will respond. That is part of the communicative equation that we as ministers don't control and have never controlled. We are called to offer the gift of our words. The ground on which the seeds fall isn't ours to determine. Despite the risks that every preacher experiences, it's far better to be people of integrity, care, and love. Isn't it far better to focus on offering the best of ourselves than to drown in the anxiety of whether everyone will like what we say and love who we are? Let's begin by knowing that no matter how faithful we are, for a variety of reasons—some having little to do with us as people—everyone won't like what we say and won't love who we are. For me and maybe for you, the struggle is to preach not to receive love, but to preach *because we are already loved by the Greatest Lover of all.*

The Place of the Bible in Preaching

Pastoral preachers have a challenging but potentially rewarding task in proclamation. They know the congregation well enough to understand its joys, fears, dreams, and disappointments. They know themselves well enough to recognize their own responses and reactions. Now, these ministers come on Sunday morning with a biblical text/s to speak a word of comfort or challenge.

All of us who are preachers use different methods as we open the Bible to prepare for Sunday morning. Most of us listen to the suggestions of others whom we respect, and then we fashion an approach to our proclamation that fits us. In many ways, what I say here is personal because it has helped me.

Several things are important to me. When I enter a biblical text, I try to listen to it as carefully as possible. I read it silently, read it out loud, and write down things that come to mind. This is the period when chaos prevails. I'm brainstorming with the text, asking questions, trying to see the interaction of characters in a story, and basically attempting to encounter the text and let it encounter me. I don't begin the process assuming the Bible is a distant book that I must somehow make relevant to our day. I recognize that the Bible was written in other times, other places, and other languages. In that sense it does have distance, and that's why the use of the biblical critical tools are essential in excavating the text.

Yet, the Bible speaks to us at another level. For example, understanding the uniqueness of a place like Corinth is vital for interpreting the two letters to the Corinthians in the New Testament. However, in many other ways the people of Corinth are like me and like you. They struggle to do church right. They can't seem to leave old ways behind. They wonder if the forgiveness of God is license instead of liberty. They try to balance the grace of God with the call to live out the virtues of love, faith, and hope. The Corinthians doubt that anyone, including Jesus, can be raised from the dead, and in the process, they lose the life-giving ramifications of the resurrection.

Are the Corinthians like us? Yes and no. The preacher sits prayerfully before the biblical text and sees the words on the page as living messages that are as contemporary as they are ancient.

A second thing I do with a biblical text is to take figuratively some people into the room where I prepare so that I can try to see the words through their eyes. Preaching can unintentionally become a self-centered process. As best as I can, I want to put on the eyes and ears of others as I read the text. Not everybody in the congregation is a white male, raised in the

South, married, with two children, and one dog. Not everyone has the same joys, needs, experiences, or love of sports that I have. In fact, contrary to my assumptions, I have even encountered some people in churches where I served who not only didn't know the difference between the "first inning" and "first quarter," but also didn't care. A constant barrage of baseball illustrations in a sermon was a little like my son-in-law trying to explain what he does as an astrophysicist. I know a telescope when I see one; I've even looked through several. I know stars; on a clear night, I'm pretty sure I can find the Milky Way. However, when Bryan tries to explain something exciting to him as an astrophysicist, I nod politely and wonder, "How much longer until the baseball game starts?"

Allowing other people to listen to a text with us is especially important in our pluralistic, multicultural world. I often marvel at the insights that preachers from the misnamed "Third World" bring to their sermons. Then I remember that so much of the Bible is written by and about people who lived on the margins of their societies. Who better to understand a "wandering Aramean" than someone who has wandered? The perspectives and voices of women have often been silenced in the proclamation of some of our faith traditions, resulting in books of sermons written by men that reflect the passions and perspectives of those men. The answer isn't to silence men. Rather, we want to expand the kinds of voices we hear, and in my preaching, I want to be as sensitive as possible to the fact that everyone doesn't think, feel, or process life exactly as I do.

A third way in which I look at a biblical text is to ask, "What does this tell us about God?" The many people today who are interested in the mystical and spiritual side of life fascinate me. Much of my education utilized the scientific method to find answers, and that approach put a high premium on the power of reason. In many ways, I was a great, great, great, etc., grandchild of the Enlightenment. Sermons I heard as a young person often set out to prove things about who God was and how God worked. A guest minister at my home church tried to prepare the high school students for college and for what he felt would be an assault on our faith. For example, he preached a sermon on creationism and why he thought that was a more reasonable option than evolution. While I don't remember the specifics of the message, I do recall seven or eight arguments that in his opinion eliminated any rational person's belief that evolution played a part in God's creation of the world.

While this minister wouldn't say it and certainly didn't intend to do it, he reduced faith to a series of propositions that he thought could be successfully argued. None of us would disagree that our faith involves propositions. I affirm certain ideas that I can state in one or two sentences. However, if we package the Christian faith into a neat set of propositions, we lose the mystery, the surprise, the stories with their asymmetry, and the wonder of our relationship with God that can be expressed but not always explained. We reduce God to our set of expectations and lose the joy of a life lived like a dance in which God always takes the lead.

Many people today seem hungry for a relationship with God. They want to know that the preacher has walked into a biblical text and emerged with more than a few stagnant points about some dimension of life. These people listen to the preacher to see if the preacher can still be amazed by God, to see if she or he can still be surprised and even stunned by the God who always exceeds our powers of reason and our polished rhetoric. The minister walks into the story of Abraham taking his son up the mountain of worship. Questions spring to the minister's mind. What is Sarah doing as her son, her only son, the son whom she loves so dearly, is taken by her husband? What is Isaac thinking? He notices his father has brought no ram to sacrifice. Does Isaac resist when he's placed on the altar? What is Abraham thinking? Abraham is the father of a new faith, the one who begins the whole journey of Israel. But is Abraham no more enlightened than people in other religions of his day who regularly sacrificed their children to appease the gods? What about Abraham's God? What is God doing? Does this God require us to offer our children to show our love?

Like so many stories and incidents in the Bible, this piece of drama is reckless and wild. It can't be easily tamed by our words. Maybe this is a story about faith and obedience, but it's irrational to any of us who care about our children and who have suffered enormously whenever our children have suffered. We begin to glimpse a God of mystery whose ways are not our ways. We come to the sanctuary to speak about God, Abraham, Isaac, and Sarah, and we have to admit that we are almost speechless as we stand before the text. I begin to understand that parts of the Bible exceed pat answers, and I don't come with easy, symmetrical responses. I come to the church house as a fellow struggler, knowing God is often a God who doesn't follow my lead. I come to tell the story with awe and amazement, and then I say that this is a God who is beyond us.

Who really wants a God that we can fully comprehend or place in the confines of our feeble words? Who really wants a God where you and I choreograph the dance of our lives and bring in the divine only to follow our lead? Who really wants a God that we have domesticated and whose will is our will and whose ways are our ways? Preaching grows timid when God is made in our image. As proclaimers, we take people into the world of the Bible and speak of a God who is big enough to have God's way and who doesn't give us easy answers in a complex and ambiguous world. We want our hearers and ourselves to experience God, to love God with mind, heart, and soul.

Our daughter recently came home for a short visit. When I picked her up at the airport, I watched her emerge from the baggage area and saw the young adult she's become. Laura Beth is working on her dissertation in New Testament. In a meaningful way, she and I are theological colleagues. We talk about cognitive matters. I love her bright mind. But, of course, I love her because she's my daughter. All of me, however you want to label the parts, loves her. I love her because she's my child. When our family is together, we experience the fullness of each other. Label that fullness "heart, mind, and soul." It's beyond description. So is God. In our world with its confusion, the minister doesn't say, "I have all the answers." We point to God and allow ourselves to experience the fullness of God's presence. "How can we know the way?" the disciples asked as Jesus was preparing them for life after the cross. Jesus personalized the reply. "I am the way," Jesus said. In preaching, we don't begin by calling people to believe ideas about Jesus. Instead, we call people to believe in Jesus. In the journey of our faith, there is not an infallible roadmap that guides us unerringly to discern all the ways of God and all the ways in which God may lead us. Jesus doesn't tell his followers "the way." He *is* the way. Jesus calls them to trust his loving preparation for the future and to move forward by faith. That way of living stays open to mystery, to surprise, and ultimately to the God who refuses to be pinned down by our desire for absolute certainty.

WHAT IS PASTORAL PREACHING?

Pastoral preaching incorporates the dynamics of any kind of preaching. However, in speaking about pastoral preaching *per se*, I see two elements that are important to emphasize. Pastors look at themselves and their congregations. What do they see? Obviously pastors see many things. They see people they know are struggling with difficult issues. They see those trying to find a meaningful faith in a time when casual belief is too thin. They see congregations that need to be challenged to act more as the church in and for the world. Just as it's easy for individuals to turn inward and to become obsessed by our concerns, sometimes a church finds itself consumed with its own survival, its own conflicts, and pours all its resources into a struggle to stay together and to keep its doors open to minister to its own constituency. Any thought of reaching the world, much less the neighborhood, is lost. Nobody dreams about the difference the church can make beyond its boundaries. The church is conceived as an address, and the focus is to maintain the place we have.

What I'd like to suggest is that pastoral preaching has two primary purposes. First, it calls people in the community of faith into a deeper, more significant relationship with God. Second, pastoral preaching calls the community named *church* into the world to make known this God who always seeks a loving connection with all people.

The Call to a Deeper Relationship with God

Some influential homileticians such as David Buttrick have been highly critical of preaching that they perceive as too individualistic and too "therapeutic." These critics make a credible point. Preaching that views the congregation as individuals who need to be spiritually and emotionally healthier can become too oriented in the direction of therapy. Frankly, this is my favorite way to preach. Highly influenced by the pastoral care movement and also by the preaching of people like Harry Emerson Fosdick, I gravitated to a view of the church that saw those who were a part of proclamation as "sick people in the hospital." Obviously, not everybody was in the intensive care unit or on life support, but I tended to see the church as folks who needed words to make them feel more encouraged, better about themselves, or at least to know that God hadn't forsaken them in their difficulties.

I'm certain that one of the reasons I enjoyed this type of preaching was the fact that this is what I wanted to hear for myself. In the selection of my sermons and in my preparation, I would take myself into the room and would ask myself, "Chuck, what do you need to hear?" Some of this was self-centered. However, my approach was heavily informed by the idea that what is most personal is most universal. The logic was that if I was struggling with self-esteem, almost everybody listening to me was also struggling with it.

This kind of preaching does draw an audience. Many of us are wounded in some way, and the minister who preaches this way will find people who want a helpful word and who also want to know that they are not alone in their struggles. Pastors who preach with this focus usually project warmth, empathy, and understanding. If done effectively, this type of preaching can create identification of the minister as a fellow pilgrim on the journey. Preachers can collapse some of the distance between listeners and themselves by preaching sermons that deal with issues common to most people.

Unlike David Buttrick, I want to affirm the value of this type of preaching. As I've mentioned, there are some dangers. It can be for the preacher both self-centered and self-serving. It has the potential to create within listeners the desire on Sunday morning to ask only, "What's in it for me?" Buttrick is certainly correct to say that "individualistic" and "therapeutic" preaching possesses serious dangers. Theologically, we turn God into the "great therapist" whose sole concern seems to be that we are happy, healthy, and emotionally stable.

Yet, with those potential problems, speaking to people where they are and trying to bring them into a deeper understanding of who God can be for them are legitimate and needed objectives of preaching. Part of our difficulty may be terminology. "Individualistic" and "therapeutic" are not as accurate as I would like. They conjure distasteful images in my mind. Individualistic implies that it's all about me. Therapeutic is often a word associated with personal psychotherapy. While many of us have been helped by individual therapy, I recognize that this is usually associated with people who have the financial resources to pay. Also, most of us as ministers are not accredited therapists. While I may speak about issues such as depression, I want to be careful that everyone who listens to me understands that my training and my calling are to preach, not to conduct psychotherapy.

Perhaps a more appropriate way to image our work as pastoral preachers is to see ourselves as calling our listeners—and ourselves—into a deeper relationship with God. For several reasons, this is more appropriate.

First, it underscores our fundamental purpose. It's not therapy; it's not social action; our primary purpose is to call our listeners and ourselves into relationship with the God revealed most completely in Jesus the Christ. Once we have been vitally connected to that God, then our task is to deepen that relationship by understanding more of who God is, who we are, and what God asks of us. We do that both individually and in community. As individuals, we want to know more of who this God is. As the community of faith, we want to know more of forgiveness, faithfulness, and love while at the same time we strive to actualize this intimate connection with God in service to the world God loves.

This means that our preaching doesn't begin with the question, "How can this message be therapeutic?" Instead, we begin by asking, "How can I present the God of the Bible in a way that all of us understand better what this God is about and wants to be about in our lives?" By no means does this suggest that the preacher comprehends and is able to articulate all that God is. At times, we need to allow people to glimpse the God that surprises, shocks, and stuns us. We need to let people know that God comforts and challenges us in ways that we probably wouldn't choose. For example, in the Sermon on the Mount in Matthew's Gospel, Jesus tells his followers to live the day they have and not worry about tomorrow because tomorrow will have troubles of its own. Surely Jesus could have been more positive. Even Annie, in the Broadway-play-turned-movie, sang more optimistically about "Tomorrow."

Yet, Jesus doesn't seem to express any kind of frothy optimism. His good news is spoken into the teeth of life where things go wrong and where people confront real problems. Similarly, those of us who are preachers deal with two visions of reality. On the one hand, we see life as it is. Hardly a week passed when I was a pastor that somebody didn't face hard, tough realities. For me to preach that "every day, in every way, life gets better and better" was to ignore what some folks were experiencing. Pain, grief, tears—these were a part of the life of Jesus, and they are a part of our lives.

To preach in a way that deepens people's relationship to God is to affirm the "other" reality. As Walter Brueggemann has said, it is to exercise "counter-imagination." In the life of Jesus, how amazing it is that he kept calling attention to the continuous presence of God. On good days, Jesus might point to the "lilies of the field and the birds of the air" to remind his disciples of the providential care of God. On Jesus' most difficult days, even the day of his crucifixion, Jesus uttered a prayer—"My God, my God, why have you forsaken me?"

These are reminders both to preachers and to our listeners that life has its rhythm. Sometimes life couldn't be any better. Like the lilies of the field and the birds of the air, we feel the joy of being cared for and loved. We wish that our lives could just ride the wave of goodness. But the reality of being human is that we live in a world where goodness and mercy may follow us, but sometimes they seem at a distance. We may pray, but we wonder if God has forsaken us.

One of the tasks of preaching is to remind us of another reality. It's not to deny the presence of evil and all the ways that evil expresses itself. Rather, this kind of preaching calls us to look more deeply and to see life as a sacred gift where epiphanies of God come in a multitude of ways. This kind of proclamation, in a sense, is "born from above" because it dares to say that the ultimate reality is God. I remember asking Fred Craddock, "What is the last thing you say to yourself before you preach?" I don't remember the exact words, but basically Craddock said he thanks God that the impact of what he says isn't based on how he feels at that moment.

Initially, I was disappointed at his answer. I don't know what I was expecting. However, the more I thought about Fred Craddock's words, the more I came to see how profound they really were. Ministers aren't immune to the rhythms of life. On Sunday mornings, the bells chime, the prelude begins, the congregation waits, and the pastor walks into the sanctuary. "To preach or not to preach, that is not the question." We preach trusting that God fills our words with power, and we dare to preach the other reality of God's presence and power. This reality has nothing to do with how we may feel at the moment. As ministers, we call our listeners and ourselves to look more deeply and to trust again that God is at work shaping us.

The Call to Be a Blessing

If preaching's only aim is to help its listeners deepen their connection to God, then we have a problem. As valid as that purpose is, it can become a highly self-centered approach to worship. This may be a particular temptation in our time. For example, seeker services or seeker-sensitive services are built on the assumption that many people in our society are hungry for an experience with God. While these services are constructed with the post-modern, post-Christian listener in mind, they often include few references to the demands of discipleship. The message focuses on some problem or need that contemporary people have and then offers suggestions from a Christian perspective about how to deal with that challenge.

The problem for this type of preaching as well as for much preaching is how do we call people beyond themselves to be the sacrificial people of God in the world? If our view of the church is that it's basically a hospital for sick people, then the temptation is to try to get people well and back on their feet but not to give them much direction about where to walk. When this happens, homileticians like David Buttrick are right. Without intention, a church becomes self-serving, therapeutic, and oriented toward the individual.

While there is ample testimony in the Bible that God is concerned about people, there is also at least equal emphasis upon the church as a community with a mission to the world. In the Hebrew Scriptures, God calls the community of Israel to receive a blessing. At the same time, that blessing is connected to the equally clear call to bless others. In the New Testament, Jesus calls individuals into a personal relationship with God. Jesus seems genuinely concerned that people know the fullness of salvation as "wholeness" in their relation to the God he reveals. Yet, community quickly forms with a band of disciples, and the Gospels generally end with Jesus' call to this "New Israel" to extend the presence of God into all the world.

The question for those of us who are preachers is not whether we will call our churches to be a blessing, but how we do it. Perhaps the beginning point is to reaffirm the presence of Christ in the world. What did Jesus mean when he said that when his followers ministered to the least of people, they ministered to him? Was Jesus saying that in the world where the church ministers—a world where we often make judgments about the good and the bad, the needy and the wealthy, the grateful and the spiteful—in each person and in all of this world, Christ is present? When we move the church into the lives of people and perform acts of mercy and kindness, we are actually ministering to the God who so loved the *world* that God gave God's "only, one-of-a-kind son...."

This gives new perspective to ministry. The church doesn't allocate its resources to those that it deems to be worthy. Those of us in the church understand that grace is a gift of God to us. The entire Christian message of salvation is built on God's doing a work in our lives that we don't earn. We are part of the family of God because God's unconditional love has broken through our resistance. Therefore, when we offer our love based on our opinion that someone deserves it, we are contradicting the very basis on which we have become children of God. We look at people not in terms of categories into which we put them or whether their behavior or lifestyle agrees with our moral codes. We see them in a new way. There is something of the Christ, the incarnated God, dwelling in them, and whether we agree or disagree with who they are or what they do, we are called to them.

A second component is to reaffirm that God is already at work in people and places in the world. The church doesn't possess God. We're not called to take the God we have to a world around us that has no God. Rather, we are called to make people aware of the God who is already at work but may not be recognized. One of the most fascinating stories in the New Testament is Luke's account of the two followers of Jesus who journey to Emmaus. It's the Sunday afternoon following the resurrection. However, these two followers aren't sure Jesus has been raised. Before leaving Jerusalem, the men heard rumors from several women who went to the burial site, saw two angels, and heard the remarkable news that Jesus had been raised from the dead. But these two followers, and for that matter nobody else, had seen Jesus alive. It's hard to base your life on rumors.

As the two followers journey to Emmaus, a stranger joins them. Luke tells his readers the stranger is Jesus. However, the men don't know that. The three walk and talk for awhile, then the two invite the stranger to spend the night since it's getting dark. In the house, the stranger takes the bread, gives thanks, breaks the bread, and in that act the stranger is "recognized." What a riveting moment. The men recognize the person who has walked with them as more than a stranger; this is the risen Savior.

The church doesn't carry the omnipresent God into the world. As preachers, we are called to point to where people's lives are broken and where injustice and inhumanity prevail and to name the God who wants to be recognized and known for who God is. This is the God who wants us to be reconciled both to God and to each other.

This approach to calling the church beyond itself recognizes that God is always beyond the church. How presumptuous of us to believe that God is only present to those of us in the church house. This is the God who loves the world, and our task is to move to where God already works and call all of us to "recognize" this God.

Several years ago there was a fervent debate in some evangelical circles about individual salvation versus the social gospel. On one side were advocates of bringing individuals to a recognition of God through faith in Jesus Christ. On the other side were people who said God is more concerned about issues of inequity and injustice. In truth, the Bible seems to indicate that God is concerned with both. At some point, those of us who follow Christ felt impressed that we were important to God. As people, we were loved by God. Those of us who were used to trying to achieve love have probably struggled most of our lives to receive the gift. For me, this grace, this unconditional love of God, is antithetical to the way I perceive life. Yet, deep down I believe this is the good news, and I will probably spend all my days trying to appropriate its fullness.

This same God of love is also deeply concerned about the welfare of all God's children. Surely, God must weep that so many people are hungry. God must weep at the incredible amounts of money nations spend to make war. God must weep at the ways we have polluted and spoiled the earth that is God's creation. God must weep when God's children are kept from using their gifts because they are women. There's so much more.

This is where God is present, and we are called to name that presence and recognize the stranger. When the two disciples saw who Jesus was, that same night they left the security of Emmaus to return to the despair that filled other followers in Jerusalem. However, when the two men returned, they voiced a new message of hope: "It is true! He is risen!"

Listening for the Sacred

As I've mentioned, those of us in ministry are put together in a multitude of ways. There's no such thing as *the minister*. We are *ministers*, and we come in different packages with different gifts, different personalities, and varying vulnerabilities. We learn about ourselves as pastors. We find the parts of our ministry that bring us the greatest satisfaction. We discover certain personality types to which we are attracted and which draw the best from us. On the other hand, we encounter people that irritate us, annoy us, and generally make us feel that it's all right for us to be paid for what we do.

Since ministers are different, it is difficult to characterize us as all having the same needs. This chapter, therefore, is written with my story in mind. In sharing with other clergy, I find that many of them can live into my story because they, too, live much the same story.

When I look at my life, I can describe it with words like "work," "achieve," "competition," and "activity." I've said that much of my journey has been done from the position of "I'm not O.K." This means several things for me. First, I've worked extremely hard to try to prove myself. Like all pastors, I've received negative criticism for some aspects of my ministry, but I don't remember being criticized for not working hard.

Second, this sense of not being O.K. has resulted in personal anxiety. Anxiety has been described as the gap between our ideal for ourselves and the reality that we actually accomplish. As a pastor, I always had extremely high expectations of my preaching. I envisioned words carefully crafted and winsomely spoken. I dreamed of hearers' lives being deeply moved. Those of you who preach know that there are relatively few times when we get within sight of the perfection we sometimes imagine. Some of my personal anxiety has lessened with the passing years, but I remember spending many Sunday afternoons berating myself for not preaching as well as I would like.

A third consequence of this "performative" approach to ministry and proclamation is the sacrifice of contemplation, meditation, and prayer. My response to my perceived failure was increased activity. I would work harder, which only increased my anxiety, my fatigue, and often my depression. Looking back, I see now the self-centeredness of this approach to ministry. It was all about me and how I was doing. Of course, I would have told you that I worked on God's behalf and that my efforts were to strengthen the church. Truthfully, I was frightened by the constant fear of failure, and my renewed efforts were a response to that fear.

One dimension of this fear may be peculiar to me, but I believe it embraces other ministers. Ministry is a difficult vocation in which to evaluate success. A church can function almost chaotically at times, and perhaps it's a sign of God's blessing that some churches do as well as they do. For some of us who are ministers, however, knowing the effectiveness of our ministry is difficult to determine. Do we decide on the basis of the number of new members? Does a building program indicate success? What about the programs a church offers? In some cases, these may be legitimate measurements, but it is difficult to measure changes in people's lives and their growth in faith.

At the seminary where I teach, I'm involved in a class with Doctor of Ministry students each year and sometimes supervise them in their projects. If you're familiar with D.Min. projects, you know that they often involve measurements and statistics. For example, a minister may decide to preach a series of sermons on a particular topic. She or he selects a sample group in the church and gathers data on the group before preaching. Following the sermons, she or he then gathers more data to see if there has been growth in understanding of the topic or commitment to the ideas of the sermon.

This is where the fun begins. How do you really measure the effectiveness of a sermon or series of messages? If I intend as a preacher to communicate information, then the statistical task is relatively easy. I measure what the listeners know before and after the sermons. If the hearer's cognitive knowledge has increased, then I can proclaim my preaching a success and give myself a good grade. However, the difficulty is to measure the transformative element in proclamation. In other words, does what people learn make any real difference in who they are as followers of Christ? Fred Craddock has said that the longest journey we ever make is from our heads to our hearts, from what we know to what we appropriate and actualize in our lives.

As a pastor I liked to see results. I wanted to know that what I did affected people's lives. I wanted to be assured that my preaching made a difference. Of course, these are the things we can't measure in any scientific way. We may rely on anecdotal information or people's telling us that what we do and say as ministers affects them positively. But almost every pastor knows what it's like to come to the end of a busy day, look back at a myriad of things we've done, and wonder if we have made any difference in our slice of the world.

How do those of us who are pastors deal with our fears, anxieties, stress, depression, and times when we wonder if what we do makes any positive difference? We need to do something because the stories are legend of ministers who do destructive things to themselves and to the work of God in the world. Of course, part of the answer may be in our seeking professional help. It's not a sign of weakness for us to see a psychiatrist if our depression makes it difficult to function. Unfortunately, pastors like myself can become isolated in our pain because we believe that any admission of need may communicate inadequacy or weakness. The problem is that we don't get the assistance we need until we have acted out our distress in some inappropriate way. The other response we sometimes take is to avoid our ministry responsibilities simply because we don't have enough energy to meet the demands. People notice that our sermons aren't as prepared and vibrantly delivered as they once were; that we don't visit the hospitals as responsibly as we once did; or that our capacity to listen to someone else is diminished by what seems to be our preoccupation with other matters. What people in the congregation may not understand is that we are tired and, perhaps, clinically depressed. That's why it's imperative that ministers not isolate themselves from professional and medical resources.

Primarily, I want to speak about our own spiritual formation as ministers. I suppose I speak about this because I recognize my own needs in this area. In teaching homiletics, I have begun to look more carefully at the close interaction between preaching and the minister's own spiritual life. I'm especially concerned about our students whose vocational goal is pastoral ministry. The work of a pastor, including preaching, can be depleting because we offer the gift of ourselves. Like Jesus in the story of the woman who touched the hem of his garment, we recognize that in offering who we are, something goes out of us. For me, preaching has always been the most satisfying but the most difficult task. I never finish a sermon without feeling that some energy, some power, some part of me has gone out. How do we replenish ourselves spiritually? How do those of us called to feed others feed ourselves so we don't perish from spiritual starvation?

STANDING IN THE NEED OF PRAYER

It's interesting for me as an interim pastor to listen to a church's leadership talk about the qualities the congregation needs in a new pastor. Of course, character issues are always important. No church looks for a duplicitous, self-centered, untrustworthy, or morally reprehensible minister. As it should, the church seeks someone who models the kind of lifestyle that serves the cause of Christ. Without calling names, we are all too familiar with well-known, glitzy preachers who took a great fall. In most cases they repented after they were caught, but all the tears and contrite words didn't undo the damage to the impression that some people have of ministers.

Let's face it. While most people respect the vocation of ministry, there are folks who suspect our intentions, distrust our pious words, and are all too eager to remind us about some of our kind who were caught with their hand in the money jar or who had a rendezvous with some woman in a seedy motel room. Frankly, I would appreciate these ministers apologizing to other ministers and not just to the people who contribute to their causes. Unfortunately, some of the most magnetic preachers seem to struggle with some of the most severe issues. We do ourselves a disservice when we take our press clippings too seriously or when the adulation of some hearers causes us to lose sight of the vulnerable parts of our humanity.

A church has every right to expect its pastor to *be* something. However, most churches fill their job description with expectations to *do*. The pastor is expected to do this or do that. Within reason, this is understandable. The pastorate is a demanding call filled with a multiplicity of tasks. Even a well-organized pastor soon discovers that not every day is the same, and he or she has to learn to deal with the unexpected. When I was a pastor, I probably averaged about one funeral a week. Pastors of older congregations average more than that. Sometimes the death of a person in the church breaks in with fierce surprise.

The first funeral at which I spoke and officiated was for an infant. I was still a college student with all the grandiose visions of the difference I would someday make as a minister. The day of that first funeral is embedded in my mind. I talked to the devastated family, led the service, read Scripture, had prayer, and said words about God's being with us and about the baby's being with God. After the service, I went back to my apartment and sat in a chair all afternoon wondering whether my words had made one shred of difference. The family had been kind to thank me for being with them, but this was their baby. I know we as pastors have to maintain some distance between ourselves and those who hurt. We can't die at every funeral. We can't get sick with every parishioner taking chemotherapy.

But let's get real. I was never able to separate myself completely from people in the church. Certain events triggered deep emotional responses in me. An elderly woman called to say she had been diagnosed with cancer. She was like another mother to me. A young woman was killed in an automobile accident. She was so winsome, so bright; she had been so alive. One afternoon I went to a house to tell parents that their son had taken his life. I asked his mother and dad to sit beside me on the couch in their family room; I said his name, and then told them their child was dead. I will never forget the looks on their faces.

I understand when ministers tell me they are depleted. It's not just the work. It's the kind of work that sometimes pulls from us the deepest feelings. Yet, there's always the regular work to be done. The sermon for Sunday morning needs to be prepared. Regardless of what we've been through that week, folks will be waiting for words from us.

How do ministers handle this? In larger churches with multiple staff, we may find the Senior Pastor's almost exclusive responsibility is to preach. The work of the church through the week, even many of the weddings and funerals, is handled by colleagues on the staff. The distance between the preaching minister and most of the congregation is large. The pastor may relate to a select few laypeople, but most of the church understands that the primary role of their minister is to preach.

Obviously, this kind of arrangement puts relatively little day-to-day stress on the pastor. As long as exciting sermons are preached, the congregation accepts that their other needs are met by a cadre of specialized ministers. While this isn't the type of pastoral leadership I like or commend, it does remind us that in a larger church context or maybe any church context, the pastor can't fulfill all the demands. Some of us with high needs to know everything or keep tabs on all that happens have a difficult time delegating and trying not to micromanage. Perhaps we need to examine our compulsion to be aware of everything, or maybe we need to examine our ecclesiology. For all of the talk about enabling and empowering others being the heart of our ministries, some of us don't trust others enough to give them confidence to minister with us.

Living out of trust or distrust is also critical in how we do our ministry. Do we trust God for ourselves? Do we perform our tasks of ministry with an awareness of God's presence? Do we see ministry as something we do for God or as something God does with and for us? Does prayer, an awareness of the divine, inform our lives on a continuous basis, or is it simply marginal to our existence as ministers?

You and I may think that the spiritual formation of the pastor is inherent in our calling. Throughout my own ministry, I think I assumed that because I was doing what I interpreted to be God's work, I could also be certain that I would stay aware of the holy. Unfortunately, that wasn't the case. In fact, vocation in the church may hinder what is sometimes referred to as "life in the Spirit."

Several factors may contribute to this. Most of us who enter ministry have a strong idealism about what the church will be and what we will be as the church's ministers. When we move into the life of the congregation, we quickly discover both people's humanity and our own humanity. People say things that hurt. Churches have to meet budgets. Leaders have personality quirks and personal conflicts. As pastors, we are confronted with our own limits. We become tired and too easily discouraged. We sacrifice our commitment to be prepared preachers, and we turn to the enticing advertisement about sermon outlines complete with illustrations that we can microwave on Saturday nights. We spend less and less time on things that can be nurturing and meaningful for us.

In my opinion, spiritual formation begins with a realistic assessment of both what the church is and who we are as ministers. The church is filled with human beings who act like human beings. People in the church can be loving, but they can also be bitter. Some folks have a wonderful vision of the church's being Christ's presence in the world. Others see it as the place to exert their power, and, thus, almost every church has its small battles and sometimes large wars.

As ministers, we mirror much of this. We love God, but we also love the affirmation of people. Some of us will avoid conflict even if it's appropriate and may prevent more complicated problems in the future. We dream wistfully of what it would be like to be the pastor of that early fellowship in the book of Acts where everybody shared, everyone loved each other, and the congregation prospered. We conveniently forget that this euphoria seemed to be short-lived. Before we know it, Ananias and Sapphira appear on the scene trying to dodge their financial pledge, and there's big trouble in "church world." If we pastors pine for a simpler, purer time when the church was really the church, maybe we need to read again Paul's letters to the Corinthian congregation or the not too complimentary word to Laodicea recorded in Revelation.

I discovered in my own ministry that I became much too dependent on positive feedback from the congregation. Even when I received a positive response, I'm not sure it ever meant as much to me as it should. Being a perfectionistic person, I wanted people to respond to me with only superlatives. Words like "good," "nice," or "fine," weren't strong enough to feed my insecurities. Think of the number of people on any given Sunday who tell their pastors, "That was absolutely the most wonderful message I've ever heard." I don't even tell other ministers that. As the lyrics of the country music song remind us, "I was looking for love in all the wrong places."

Once in awhile I did receive a response that approached the adoration I wanted. Do you know what those comments did to me? They frightened me. After all, if this Sunday's sermon is the best, what do you do for next Sunday's message? Those of us who are perfectionistic, competitive, and highly dependent on the praise of others are caught on a treadmill that keeps going faster. How do we slow ourselves down? How do we recover a sense of self so that what we do as ministers is born from gift and not from need?

Desperation can cause us to do strange things. I began to remember times when I felt so much more intimate with God. I recalled moments when I had begun my journey of faith with the Christ of God and how reassuring his love and closeness were to me. Obviously, I couldn't go back in time. Too much had taken place. In some ways, I was a different person. But here was the catalyst that moved me, as Frederick Buechner says, to the "room called Remembrance." While I was different from that boy who had come to faith, in so many ways I was the same. I was more educated, more aware that life can't be as easily explained as I once thought. I had been a pastor. My illusion that people always acted with the best of themselves had disappeared. I became more realistic.

Yet, at a profound level I had not really changed all that much. When I came to faith in Jesus Christ, I remember how reassured I was to know that God loved me and was present to me. I needed that. At the time, I wouldn't have used the word "anxiety," but that would have described how I felt much of the time. I worried about whether I was accomplishing or achieving enough. I measured myself by grades in school, athletic accomplishments, or whether I was elected captain of the safety patrol or president of the student council. If I accomplished something, I temporarily felt good about myself. But the question was always in my mind: If I failed or even did an average job, would I be loved or would I love myself? I knew the answer to the second part. No! I would second-guess myself, feeling I needed to put forth more effort.

How empowering it was for me to experience the presence of a personal, loving God. Could I recover that after so many years? Had I become too much the pastor? Had I seen too much of life's complexity? Had I become so analytical about my vocation, including God, that I could no longer regain that childlike trust and wonder? Those were serious concerns. We've all been with children and reveled in their delight in life. One evening, I entered a church where I was interim pastor. A little boy sat on the stairs trying to tie his shoe. Attempting to be the Good Samaritan, I sat next to him and said, "Do you want me to help you?" As he fumbled with the strings, the boy shot me a glance that let me know my help was not wanted or needed.

Without overanalyzing this experience, I think the child and I saw "shoe-tying" in two different ways. As the adult, I saw a problem that needed a solution. The best solution was for me to tie his shoes so we could all get on to our next commitment. What I missed was this little boy's need to tie his own shoes, even if he had to sit on that step for another hour. After I excused myself, I told my wife, "Do you know I forgot how important it used to be for me to tie my own shoes?" They didn't have a perfect bow. Often, they would come untied because I didn't have a tight knot. Most important, though, was the wonder of doing it myself. I wasn't thinking about getting to the next meeting on time. For a few moments, life was so good, so wonderful, so beautiful because I had tied the laces on my shoes.

How do we become childlike again? Interestingly, an approach to looking at Scripture became the opening for me. Paul Ricoeur calls it the "second naiveté." It's when we open a biblical text, read it, and then let it read us as if we meet the words for the first time. How important this is for pastors. My tendency is to view the Bible as the "source book" for my sermons. Since I have familiarity with the Bible, I may scan or halfheartedly read the biblical text from which I preach. I assume I already know what it says. Instead of opening the Bible and standing before the text with a feeling of wonder, with the throttle of my imagination wide open, I open the Book so I can get the content and contours of my sermon.

How refreshing it's been to see myself first and foremost as the listener to the biblical text. To be able to sit in front of the words of Scripture and to try to hear the message of challenge or comfort has renewed my own passion for the Bible. The call to preach is to have something to say, not just to say something, as someone has wisely said. The little boy tying his shoelaces didn't seem to be in any hurry to go somewhere else. Tying his shoes was the thrill and the challenge of the moment, and the last thing he wanted was some overly unctuous, codependent minister messing up the wonder of that achievement.

For whatever success or failure I have experienced as a minister, what I had left behind was what I really needed the most. I needed to know that the God whose name I so often invoked loved me. As John Claypool has said, "I needed to know that the waters of grace could sustain the weight of my being." I needed to trust. I needed that childlike dependence that had first brought me to God, and I needed to admit that I was lonely, frightened, and standing in the need of prayer.

Those who try to study the art of preaching know that there has been a new surge of interest in "reader-response criticism." Older types of biblical criticism assumed that the meaning of a biblical text was within the words of Scripture, and the task of the preacher was to uncover the "gem" of meaning. Now we talk more seriously about the "relational" nature of Scripture. I come to the text with who I am, and the truth happens in my encounter with the text. This approach assumes that a biblical text is polyvalent. It is open to multiple meanings, all of which may be true to me depending on who I am and what I'm experiencing. Reader-response criticism, for instance, takes seriously the way a black woman who has known the oppression of race and gender reads a passage of Scripture, and how that differs from a white man who's experienced a certain authority and acceptance simply because of who he is.

While reader-response criticism alone can result in a kind of hermeneutical subjectivity, it does remind us that the deepest truth we know is a happening and connecting truth. We don't simply nod our heads to affirm something as true and then leave it, as if truth has its own room in the house of our being that we visit as our schedule allows.

Again, this has been a most helpful model for me to see again the strength of God in relationship. Ministers "study" God. We are fascinated by new ideas. We study the church. We read books about new forms for doing church, for worship, and for structuring new ways to be alive to the challenges of the new millennium. We analyze our faith. The problem is that if all we do is analyze, we build into ourselves the inevitable distance between subject and object. While that may work in some vocations, it is devastating to ministry because it distances us from the very God who is the "source" of our being. Truth has an objective quality. We can find definitions for love, for example. However, do we really know all that love is until we experience it in relation to another? We may not be able to define that experience as clearly as someone on the outside would like, but we can describe the joy, pleasure, and fulfillment we feel in the presence of the beloved.

SEEING ALL OF MINISTRY AS GIFT-GIVING

One of the inherent difficulties in congregational ministry is the wide variety of tasks a minister is called to perform. Complicating the issue is that many of these tasks seem so divergent. We also have to factor into this already complicated equation our expectation that we will be able to do everything well. One of the things I often felt and I've heard other ministers express is an overwhelming sense of fatigue. We even talk about the problem of "clergy burnout."

What causes this fatigue? Obviously, a multitude of factors can contribute. Some of us never allow ourselves a Sabbath. Our need to be needed keeps us running from one job to the next. For us, there is never a seventh day. Other ministers don't take care of themselves physically. We may overeat, eat the wrong things, or never give ourselves permission to exercise. These are some of the things that contribute to a minister's fatigue. The work of a pastor is intrinsically busy and involves physical, mental, emotional, and spiritual investment.

Those of us with the opportunity to speak to churches need to remind our listeners that the combination of an overexpecting congregation and overexpecting pastor is an invitation to conflict, frustration, and ultimately the fracturing of the relationship. However, as we speak to churches about excessive demands, we need to be honest with those who feel called to church ministry that it is a serious personal investment. Those who feel called must recognize the human side of ministry. They must be willing to give themselves to a vocation where the fruits of their work aren't always seen and where people who've never been to a seminary will be more than willing to critique everything they do. I say this not to discourage people from following the call of God into the church. Rather, I want to guard against the naiveté that some have when they become pastors and the tragic consequences of disillusionment both for clergy and the church.

With that said, I want to focus on part of the whole issue. I find this certainly true of me. Much of the fatigue I have felt can be attributed to a combination of elements. I have a high need to please people and to be liked. I know that people have many expectations of me as their pastor. Therefore, I tend to become "other-directed" in the formation of my ministry and to see my life as a kind of billiard ball bouncing from one side of the table to the other. Sometimes I feel "out of control." Sometimes I feel that my ministry becomes one of responding or reacting to perceived needs.

In past situations, my inclination was to blame and to become angry with the church. "They're doing this to me," I would say. I felt fatigued not only because I was busy, but because I felt my busyness was the product of others' demands. While the work of ministry is demanding, it becomes even more demanding if pastors feel little or no control over our schedules or as if we are driven by the expectations of others.

Hindsight is so much clearer than anticipating a challenge and being ready for it. Churches can be and often are demanding in their expectations of the pastor, but those of us who think we can do it all exacerbate the problem. I wish that I had been more honest with congregations about both my gifts and my weaknesses. As with most ministers, I believe there are some facets of the ministry that I do well and some things that bring me fulfillment. I realize that a pastor can't do only what she or he enjoys. However, I would have served my congregations and myself better if I had been willing to admit the parts of the ministry in which I didn't do well. Many times I needed the help of the church.

That would have enabled me to be a more effective preacher. I would have focused more on the delights of being a pastor. I also would have modeled an essential component of a theme on which I often preached—the grace of God and how that grace becomes real as we open ourselves to the gift from beyond us. Many times I spoke about the freedom that finally comes when we admit we can't do life by ourselves, finally allowing God and the people of God to give us their strength. Despite my own words, I tried to offer too many gifts, even gifts that I didn't have.

One Saturday I went to the store and felt particularly generous. I decided I would buy a little surprise gift for everyone in the family, including the dog. I was proud of my extravagant spirit as I drove home with bags filled with gifts for everyone. After all, it wasn't Christmas or anybody's birthday. I anticipated my reception at home. Everyone would be impressed with my thoughtfulness, and while I would say, "It's just a little something," I knew! I knew that everyone, maybe even the dog, would think how caring and sensitive I was. My problem was carrying all those little bags from the car to the house. I hit my leg as I closed the car door. I dropped pieces of candy and dog biscuits on the sidewalk. By the time I got into the house, I was in a bad mood. "Why didn't anybody help me? Nobody ever helps me. I did all this for you, and now I have a bruised leg."

Do you know what? I think I tried to give too many gifts and ended up giving my frustration. What I wanted to be an occasion of delight turned into a disaster. Everybody in the family—including the dog—had to retrace my steps to find their treats while I put a cold compress on my bruised leg.

I could have handled the situation in several different ways. I might have said, "No gifts for anyone else. Life is about me. I'm not going to spend my money. After all, I could hurt myself trying to carry these bags when the gifts are not even for me." Or I could have brought the gifts to the house one at a time. That would have made more sense. I wouldn't have tried to hold more than I could handle. Or I could have bought a gift for one person. My family would have understood if I'd said, "This is the dog's day." The rest of the family wasn't expecting anything anyway. But you know what some of us want to do. We want to give gifts to everybody, even if we give to impress our recipients with our generosity.

What if we saw our ministries as simply sharing our gifts without being overly concerned with whether everyone liked us? What if we celebrated God's gifts to us and then saw our calling as the living out of what God has lived into us? I deeply believe that this approach to preaching would have alleviated much of the fatigue and anxiety I experienced. At times, I would feel threatened by a colleague with an appealing ability to preach. How sad that something like that would keep me from caring for another minister, and how tragic that I would see preaching as the event in which I had to prove my worth week by week.

Sometimes, as a pastor I would go home on Sunday afternoons tired and ready to quit because I hadn't performed as well as I had wanted. I saw preaching horizontally. For me, it was the time to shine. If you are a preacher, you understand that we preach at our absolute best on relatively few occasions.

This is why the spiritual formation of ministers is so integral to the way I teach preaching. I want all of us to be as effective as possible at communicating. If our patterns or idiosyncrasies interfere with our proclamation, I want us to be aware of those and try to change them. I do want to be conscious of our listeners, and I realize that preaching seeks to have words heard and lives changed. Yet, I don't want to turn the preaching event into such an introspective and negatively critical process. If I can help a student (or myself) better understand that we are gifts from God and each of us has gifts to give, then I will have made considerable progress on the journey to learn.

As preachers, we need to pray. Prayer is not just a reminder of who God is but of who I am. I come to God in prayer because I am a person with both gifts and limits. I am someone who sins and falls short of what God desires. At times, I think the wrong thing, say the wrong thing, and do the wrong thing. I'm not coming to God because I have gotten all of life right and just need to get my grade. Rather, I most often come to God with some goodness and some badness. The remarkable thing is that God loves me for who I already am, not for what I wish I was. This becomes the perspective from which we live. God loves us not because of what we bring to the relationship, but because God sees us as God's creation, and what we are has value.

We approach our ministry and our preaching from the same stance. We should not preach to elicit love either from God or from others. Frankly, I think God is probably amused that we preachers think so much hinges on our abilities. We fret about how well we're doing; we read a magazine, and some writer decides in a cover story who is the greatest preacher in America. I have a hunch that the greatest preacher in the United States lives in Nebraska and never received an honorary doctorate, but week by week opens the Bible and helps his/her listeners understand how the words can shape their lives.

I've spent a good portion of my ministry trying to produce, please, and preach at least well enough to get some recognition. When we do life that way, we never get enough responses to satisfy us. We are always driven to do better and be better. We imagine that one day we will feel satisfied, but that time never seems to come. We search for unconditional love when the source of that love is already within us. What if we could preach from the source? What if Sunday by Sunday we spoke as people who say through our words and lives that giving is the most meaningful way to live?

TAKING TIME TO HEAR

In a recent survey done by a member of the American Academy of Homiletics, it was reported that the average minister spends about three hours a week reading books other than the Bible. Since the amount of time reading the Bible wasn't all that impressive in the survey, the obvious conclusion is that we as ministers are not reading enough. Since we are called to preach sermons, facilitate Bible studies and devotionals, and give other presentations, this means some of us are giving out more than we're receiving.

Obviously, this affects our preaching, but another important problem is our diminished spiritual growth. Our reading is not simply a way to gather more sermon ideas or illustrations; it stretches our thinking, expands our imagination, thrusts us into other worlds, and allows us to see dimensions of living that we wouldn't normally experience. We see life through the eyes of other observers and hear it interpreted through the voices of others.

This is particularly important since pastors serve as the "frontline" theologians for congregations. Thinking theologically isn't an option for preachers. It's the heart of our call. We are not in the pulpit simply to tell cute stories, to offer advice, or to reassure people in bad times that the sun rises after the darkest part of the night. Those all may be helpful, but the primary purpose of the preacher is to try to put a divine frame around life and to speak about the biblical God whose "modus operandi" is to intersect with the lives of people like us. This requires imagination on the part of the preacher. When I talk about imagination, I'm not speaking about fantasy. I'm not making up something untrue or speaking as if none of us experience pain. Imagination isn't a plastic substitute for the hard and harsh realities of life. Our listeners quickly know when we preach as if the truths of faith are always easily understood and lived.

Rather, imagination is the ability to see the depths of life or the breadth of a biblical passage so that we can communicate the full aliveness of what we hear. Our words aren't flat. As preachers we speak from and about wonder, awe, joy, struggle, suffering, and countless other things because we see, hear, smell, and sense them in every way as we encounter a biblical text. Good writers help us develop this kind of imagination. They help us open our senses and bring to our sermons a passion that comes from experiencing a text rather than just reading it.

Look at Jesus' experience with Martha, Mary, and Lazarus in John 11. We smell death. We feel anger. "If you had been here," Martha says, "my brother would not have died!" We see the binds of life until our Lord says,

"Loose him." Most profoundly, we watch Jesus weep. Why are you crying, Jesus? Perhaps because Lazarus died. Even if he is resuscitated, in that moment Jesus tastes what it's like to live in a world where things change and people die. Maybe Jesus cried because his relationship with three people who seemed to be closest to him faced its greatest strain. The house in Bethany was his house. The home of Mary, Martha, and Lazarus had become a home and a haven for Jesus, who didn't seem to have many places to call home. Or could it be that Jesus wept because he realized more than ever that he would never truly be accepted by many of those to whom he had come? After seeing Jesus raise Lazarus from the dead, the authorities decided this was all they would tolerate from Jesus. From this moment on, Jesus' fate is sealed, and the cross casts its foreboding shadow across the remainder of Jesus' days.

Or Jesus' tears may have come from all of these things and other things that we may not even know. Frederick Buechner reminds us to pay attention to our tears. What makes us cry? It is usually an accumulation of events. Shortly after my daughter left for college, I sat in the family room of our house. I was alone. A television commercial came on. A father gave his daughter her own American Express card as he prepared to send her to college. That simple scene touched me so deeply that I started to cry. Why? My daughter is in college, and life changes. Four years before she left, our son was diagnosed with a brain tumor. His life and our family's life had not been the same. I realized that during David's surgery and radiation treatments, I had never cried. I had tried to hold myself together so we could make it through the crisis. Now, like the prick of a pin, this commercial opened the place of my tears, and for many reasons I cried.

We read the Bible with imagination, and we don't encounter flat plains. The library of the Bible is filled with hills and valleys, with faith and fear, with courage and cowardice, with joy and weeping. We find ourselves living the lives of the characters. With imagination, the distance between us and people who lived in another time and place is collapsed. We become Adam and Eve trying to shift the blame. We are Sarah surprised by what God places into our lives when we don't expect it. We are Jonah struggling to rid ourselves of the biases that keep us from authentic love.

We are Peter and Judas, Paul and Lydia. We are mother, father, sister, brother, child, and we form bonds with people whose lives are more like ours than we ever imagined. But to preach with this streak of imagination enlivening our words and our phrases, we have to listen, hear, and try to pay attention to our lives. As a minister, I sometimes ask myself, "What is the voice to which you give your greatest attention?" Is it the voice of God? Is it the voice of a writer whose sensitivity to the world sharpens my own sensitivity? Is it the voice of the homeless man who often stands at the exit of a nearby Wal-Mart store with a ragged cardboard sign that says, "Hungry . . . Need Food"? Or do I listen to the voice of the cynic inside me that says, "If I gave him money, he would spend it on a bottle of cheap wine"? Or maybe I listen too much to the voices of those who I believe will give me a blessing.

Around Thanksgiving one year, a woman came forward during an invitation hymn. She gave me the blessing of kind words and then said, "I'm a single mother. This is a difficult time of the year for me. Pastor, would you say a prayer for me and for other single mothers?" How often I've tried to remind myself and the people that I teach to take a variety of folks with us into the room as we prepare a sermon. I'm married. I've never been divorced or separated. I was in love with a girl named Sara Jane when we were both in first grade. One day she hit me over the head with a stick, and suddenly love was all gummed up with blood and tears. That's the little I've experienced personally of the pain of romance. However, when this single mother asked me to pray for her and others, in my mind the whole room became crowded with people who in some way had a dream that was crushed.

How much more I need to pay attention. Thomas Merton once talked about the world's being transparent and how through the transparency we see God. In times when I have truly looked and listened, life is richer and my preaching is more connected to where people are in their lives. When I don't listen and look, I know something essential is missing. I miss the depths of life. I don't usually hear the laughter or the crying. I don't see the loneliness or the lostness. Unlike the father in the parable of the prodigal son, I retreat into the house instead of staying in the land of hope and scanning the horizon, listening to my own heart and the hearts of others.

I suspect this is the reason I have been so drawn to the writings of Father Henri Nouwen. He makes himself so vulnerable. Vulnerability must have opened Nouwen to the rejection of those who were threatened by this much exposure of one's struggles. Yet, for many of us, Nouwen has been a gift from God. He sees some of our stirrings. Nouwen helps us name the blessings and the burdens. Then he gently guides those of us who preach to a new kind of proclamation. "Pastor, pray for me and the other single mothers who are here." In that moment, the place of worship became much more sacred. This woman would never believe she was an angel. However, if an angel is someone who brings us a message we need to hear, then she was an angel.

Does Pastoral Preaching Make a Difference?

Most theological disciplines are in a constant state of reexamination. The area of New Testament, for example, has been affected by a new quest to understand the historical Jesus. The famous or infamous Jesus Seminar drew well-known New Testament scholars together. Moving through the four Gospels, they pulled out their colored pens and offered their conclusions about what Jesus probably said or didn't say, or what they believed later redactors and editors inserted. Underlying this effort was the desire to get a more accurate picture of how Jesus understood himself. Was he an itinerant teacher with an unusual charisma that drew people to him and to his words? Was Jesus a healer and miracle worker catapulted by overzealous followers into the role of Messiah? Or was Jesus the unique revelation of God as the church has usually contended?

Theology is another changed discipline, especially in the way it is taught. Do we teach theology systematically or historically? Or do we, as many feminist scholars have reminded us, take more seriously the narrative flow of the biblical revelation? After all, the Bible is not a library of neatly arranged topics in which we study the doctrine of God, the doctrine of sin, and so forth. The Bible offers us the rich interplay of people who are good and bad, faithful and unfaithful, and who profess to love God but are often seduced by evil.

This narrative methodology has pushed some of us who process information in linear ways to think again about the kind of reductionism we do with biblical texts. My own study of the Bible has been enriched enormously by seeing stories of the Bible in terms of their movement and not just as fodder for a few deductive sermon points. Narrative preaching and narrative theology have caused us to look more carefully at story contours and to preach them as though we were a part of the stories ourselves.

Like many churches, the church where I have been interim pastor has a traditional Thanksgiving service on the Wednesday night before Thanksgiving. Young people are home from college, families are together, music fills the service, and members of the church express words of gratitude. I'm supposed to bring a message. I'm thinking—we are here, but in a sense we aren't here. We're anticipating tomorrow. Some dread Thanksgiving Day because this hasn't been a year for which they are especially grateful. During the period when the congregation shares, so many words focus on the United States, the world, and the horrific events of September 11, 2001. As pastors, we never preach to minds that are mere blank slates simply waiting for our ideas. However, on certain occasions we know that it is particularly difficult to hear anything ponderous because cups already run over with heaviness. I chose my biblical text for that night several months before the service—Philippians 4:4-7. It's typical of a Pauline letter. It's the advice section. Paul tells us to rejoice, to know the Lord is near, and to pray with thanksgiving, and he reminds his listeners of other vital components of their life in Christ.

That night, I thought about the effective prison ministry of the church. Each week a group of members visits certain prisons, and the care and compassion they show have made a significant difference. "Suppose we all met here one night as a group," I began the message, "ready to go to the prison. We were going to give them our ministry. However, when we arrived at the prison, we were asked to take a seat." Then I asked them to imagine that Paul, the prisoner, the one in shackles, walks out to tell us how to be free in Christ and how to live with the peace of Christ. I didn't even begin to talk about every word in Philippians or every idea the writer expresses. Instead, I wanted all of us churchgoers that night before Thanksgiving to experience the irony of a prisoner on the inside telling those on the outside how we can be free in Christ. I wanted all of us, myself included, to be on the receiving end. Paul didn't seem to find it necessary to define terms. Rather, life-changing words like *rejoice, pray, thanksgiving,* and *peace* tumble over each other, giving us the impression that the writer of the letter was reminding the hearers that our relationship with God is known more by description than definition. In fact, Paul seems to discourage the analytical approach by saying that the peace of God transcends all human understanding.

As all of us who are preachers know, there is a time to define, but there is also the time to delight in the story and to experience it rather than rushing to try to explain what we really can't explain anyway. Our faith has an element of mystery. The sadness of fundamentalism for me isn't its search for certainty. I agree that each of us needs to believe some things are true. Perhaps we all need to be reminded that our faith isn't shapeless. Whatever we may call them, we have doctrines or beliefs that guide us. It's hard to imagine living where everything is relative and nothing in our lives is sacred or holy. However, narrative preaching reminds us that we need the experience of God as the Holy Other, as the one who is always beyond definition and who can't be confined to creeds or captured by confessions of faith. We are on a journey, and on that journey we see new things, we hear the voices of others, and we are always open to the surprises of a God whose thoughts are not always our thoughts and whose ways are not always our ways.

This focus on reading the Bible with what many African-American preachers call "sanctified imagination" may seem a strange way to introduce a chapter on whether pastoral preaching makes a difference. However, I know myself as a pastor. Those times when I didn't consider my study of the biblical text an "adventure," I reflected a "here we go again" mentality about preaching. If the biblical word wasn't somehow born again in me, it didn't have much life when I tried to speak about it. It didn't seem to get born again or born for the first time in the lives of the listeners. Pastors know that there are times when the rhythms of our calls can become a deadening routine. We have to keep the fire burning. One of the ways I combat the fatigue and anxiety of wondering whether I'm making a difference is to allow Holy Scripture to be the fresh, present expression it was intended to be.

CREATING A NEW WORLD

I'm going to make a statement that may seem far-fetched. Over a period of time, I believe a faithful pastor/preacher can create a new world in which people see life with a totally different perspective. I'm not talking about removing ourselves from the culture in which we live. Too much preaching already does that—the kind of preaching that identifies the enemies of culture, names the targets of our displeasure, and identifies the Christian life largely as the avoidance of these things.

I have watched my own denomination, the Southern Baptist Convention, move in this direction. It's been sad, painful, and at times embarrassing to watch the group in which I came to faith and was nurtured become increasingly negative and at times inconsistent in its positions. For example, several years ago a Southern Baptist Convention resolution identified the Walt Disney Corporation as the enemy. The rationale was that Disney had drifted from its original family moorings in some movies and in some of the programs it sponsored through television subsidiaries. The fact that Disney permitted Gay Pride Day in its theme parks was also offered as a reason for the resolution.

I'm certain that there are some things the Disney Corporation sponsors with which I would disagree. However, the new in-your-face, countercultural spirit that pervades some proclamation today and gives rise to these kinds of resolutions seems out of proportion to the problem. Why stop with Disney if this is our line of reasoning? Sea World, for example, is a subsidiary of Anheiser-Busch. Certainly, we are against the damage that excessive drinking of alcoholic beverages causes. Ask a mother whose child a drunken driver has killed. Is she more concerned with Disney's permitting gay and lesbian people a day at Disney World or with the empty place at her dinner table?

Identifying the enemy so clearly does give us something to be against— if that is our need. However, it fails to see all the places in life where people of God offer themselves as salt and light. Recently, one of the presidents of a conservative Southern Baptist seminary stated that the God of Christians was not the God either of the Muslims or the Jews. Even those of us who believe deeply in evangelism wonder if this public statement, which reflects a lack of respect for two faith traditions, doesn't do far more harm than good. If I were Jewish, I would be offended at the arrogance of such a claim. If this seminary president's purpose was to create a climate for sharing our faith, in my opinion he badly missed the mark. Such demagoguery lacks the kindness and grace that is more attractive than judgment and self-righteousness. His kind of rhetoric will inflame the passions of those who like to know clearly and exactly what is right and wrong. I seriously question, though, if it makes the Christian faith more appealing to someone who is Muslim or Jewish.

So when I talk about creating a new world through preaching, I'm not talking about identifying who and what we perceive as the enemies. I'm struggling to understand what Jesus means when he tells his followers that we are "in the world" but not "of the world." Is Jesus saying that we live as residents of one kind of world, but we exist in that world with a different attitude, a different spirit, and a different sense of what is important?

It seems to me that some preaching never connects with people because it fails to recognize many of the realities of the world in which you and I live. We preach to single moms. We speak to dropout dads. We try to touch the lonely, the anxious, and the depressed with our words. At the same time, we preach to people for whom this world is good. They are happy, successful, and loved. They really aren't attentive to preachers whose sermons presume, "You just think you're happy, successful, and loved. Wait until I finish with you. If you don't feel guilty about feeling so good, I'll do my best to destroy your house of happiness."

I thought about this need that some of us preachers have to make people feel bad before we try to make them feel good. I was at a fast-food restaurant several weeks ago. Nearby was a group of five fellows, several of whom had on Harley-Davidson motorcycle T-shirts. Their arms were tattooed, and they had hair in ponytails with bandannas around their heads. I was sitting at my table dressed in my standard minister's uniform. I get my hair cut once every three weeks. Every dress shirt I own is button-down. I had on a striped tie with khaki pants. In other words, I looked completely "establishment."

The guys in the T-shirts with the thick arms and tattoos seemed to be having a good time. On the other hand, I was by myself, stirring my soup and moving the tuna fish sandwich around on my plate. What do I do? Walk over to their table and say, "I hear the laughter, but I know you really aren't happy. Don't you want to be button-down like me? Why drive a Harley with the breeze blowing through your hair when you could have a Toyota Corolla?"

I decided not to do that for several reasons. First, all of those fellows at the other table were bigger than I am. Second, they really didn't look as if they would enjoy button-down shirts. Third, who was I to say that they weren't happy and content? I could use the relatively little Greek I know and try to tell them the difference between happiness on a Harley and Jesus' notion of blessedness. But do you really think that's what they wanted and needed?

What are we trying to do for people and to people in our preaching? Perhaps Jesus gives us a strong clue in the sermons he preached. Notice Jesus didn't approach the men fishing and say, "I know you really don't like what you're doing. I know deep down you are unhappy with the life you have so I want you to leave your nets and come follow me." We read into the text our own assumptions when we conclude that Simon was miserable as a fisher-man. We play havoc with Jesus' call to follow him when we assume that everybody who follows Jesus has to feel that life has no meaning. While fish-ing isn't my fulfillment, I know some people who would be very happy if they could fish and make a living.

In fact, the case could be made that saying yes to the call to follow Jesus complicated all the disciples' lives. What Jesus offers isn't constant ecstasy. The call to discipleship isn't the call to instant gratification. Jesus doesn't give us God's everything for our nothing. I suspect the lives of the disciples would have been less confusing if they'd said no to the stranger who wanted to replace their fishing for fish with fishing for people. For example, there's abundant evidence especially in Mark's Gospel that those who followed Jesus had little understanding of their mission and task. Yet, as baffling as this journey was to them, they stayed, and from the ashes of misunderstanding rose a community of faithfulness to the anointed one.

In his preaching and teaching, Jesus seems to paint vividly a new life, a new worldview with values that at many points are contrary to the standard ways of seeing life. Certainly, Jesus' message presumes the sins of each of us and all of us. In some encounters, like his meeting with the Samaritan woman at the well, Jesus senses an emptiness that drives someone to fill that vacuum with relationships where that person is used and uses others to meet his or her needs.

However, Jesus' fundamental message isn't that we are all miserable and need him to give us the happiness we want. The message is bolder. Jesus paints a new world. He calls it the kingdom, the reign of God. It's a world within our world. While following Jesus holds the promise of eternal life, this new worlds starts for us when we begin our journey of faith. The values of this new reign are qualities like selfless love and trust in God's provision and power. In the light of God's presence, we see our own weakness, but par-adoxically, we find new strength to live and to be a witness for this caring God in a world we are called to love. This love has no boundaries. It extends to all, and the church is called to bear witness to everyone.

The message isn't that in Christ we are called to be content, happy, and at peace with ourselves. We may consider ourselves to be fortunate, success-ful, and to have so much that to contain it we have to build bigger and bigger barns. We are content. We may say that God has blessed us. But if the aim of our lives is to have and to hold what we possess or simply to share

not preaching to change statue — gift from God through us — what do I give them some of it with people who look like us, think like us, and act like us, then, as Jesus says, "We may gain the whole world but lose our souls."

Preaching demands the courage to call us to true conversion, to a vision of a new world/kingdom that Jesus gives us. What if we choose to scale back the demands of discipleship and substitute a kind of religion that endorses our self-centeredness and a way of life that revolves around our own acquisitiveness? Well, as preachers, we may keep our jobs if that is our objective. However, we may already see the inevitable problems this focus creates for the church. Many of us in ministry have complained about the countless energy and time we spend trying to keep the ship of the church afloat. We preach on stewardship because the church needs more people to give. We preach on people's getting involved because the Bible school is understaffed or the nursery needs more workers. In too many churches, the pastor often feels reduced in his/her role because that minister is focused on keeping the institution of church alive. We beg, cajole, and plead with people to assume the commitment that we thought each of us had made when we came to faith.

This is a critical time in the life of the church and in the lives of those called as pastors. What we are doing doesn't seem to be satisfying to some of us. We may keep our jobs, but the fact is that some ministers are counting the days until retirement. Other pastors either opt out or live out their ministries in quiet desperation. Not nearly enough of our best, brightest, and most committed young people are giving their lives to ministry in the church. Somehow, we have to recapture the dream of the real difference that Christ can make. Churches and their ministers must see again that the role of the preacher should not be plugging holes that spring leaks or begging us to be what we already are and do what we should do. We need to see this new reign of God and be captured by a vision that reminds us we are new creatures in Jesus the Christ.

CARING FOR THE WORLD WE HAVE

Preaching is an invitation to the brave new world that Jesus called the kingdom of God. As pastors, we call ourselves and our listeners to the conversion of priorities and perspectives toward life. At the same time, we are called to care for the church and for ourselves and to accept what we may not be able to change. There is great truth in the prayer Reinhold Niebuhr first prayed that is now called "The Serenity Prayer": "Lord, help us to change the things we can, to accept the things we cannot change, and the wisdom to know the difference."

As preachers, we want to make a difference. We want our lives to count for something. Our idealism calls us to see what can be and to proclaim a new faith for life, a new hope in life, and a new love that moves through the church and out of the church into all of God's creation. As pastors, we have to work hard to maintain this heightened sense of awareness and imagination so our preaching retains its passion. Negative criticism, excessive demands, failure to nurture our relationship with God—all of these and other things can dull the dream. We lose the passion to preach about the God who works in reckless ways, and our words become stagnant as our sermons become predictable. We expect our sermons to make no difference, and for the most part, we are not disappointed. At times, I have asked myself on the way to the pulpit, "Chuck, you're going to preach about something. Suppose you were able to appropriate that 'something' as a part of your life. Would it really make a profound difference to you?" If the answer is no, then the sermon is too small. The great vision of God isn't spoken.

The preacher lives between the land of the vision and the reality of where most of us live. For many of us, this is tough territory to negotiate, both in our understanding of the ministry and in the balance of our preaching. We are called to say two things to people. We challenge everyone, including ourselves, with the possibilities of a world where people take God seriously. We speak about new values, new purpose, and newness of life. However, we also speak words that embrace the human struggle. None of us—no church, no layperson, no ordained minister—ever embraces the new life completely. We are a strange mixture of the old and new, and sometimes a preacher has to accept the reality of people, including himself or herself, who live beneath the ideal.

If we drew a line with idealism and realism at opposite ends, where would you and I as ministers fall on the spectrum? If we are accepting people, we probably can accommodate many failings from others and ourselves. The good part of this approach is that we seldom get frustrated or angry at the way life is. We tolerate problems in the church because, after all, "That's the way people are." The downside of this attitude is that the overly accepting preacher often lacks the spark to challenge people to a significant change. Assertive laypeople in the church may see their pastor as too casual about what they consider to be important issues. An overly accepting pastor speaks in mellow and soothing ways.

At the other end of the continuum is the highly idealistic preacher. Nobody, including the minister, follows Jesus closely enough, and the intent of every sermon is to challenge. Some people are drawn to this type of proclamation. These folks will tell you they want a straightforward and vibrant preacher. Of course, these same people would also say that they prefer their preacher to attack the failings of others rather than their own. This type of preacher is passionate but also subject to frustration, anxiety, and anger. I don't prove I'm a good high jumper by setting the bar at ten feet and then requiring all of us either to jump that height or quit the team. I'm sure Jesus could jump that height if he cared, but I'm equally sure there has never been a day in my life when I ever had a chance to get that far off the ground.

Thus, I want to make a case for acceptance. I want to speak a word for pastors learning to live with things that can't or won't be changed. Pastors who envision themselves as the daring prophetic voice ripping into the staid institutions of the church undoubtedly hear words like acceptance and interpret them as compromise or even capitulation. However, I'm concerned about producing pastors who will be able to stay in ministry long enough to make a difference. I want pastors who have the fortitude to address issues of injustice and inequality. I want pastors whose primary concern is not whether their hearers will like them. Even so, I believe I know churches well enough to understand that some changes are difficult and that there will be some pockets of resistance that preaching will never penetrate.

Part of the reason I know this is that I know how difficult it is for me to change things about myself. Recently, I was in an interim pastoral situation where a committee interpreted a minor personnel policy. This change, which involved me, was communicated to me by e-mail. Frankly, I think the committee mishandled the issue. When I received the e-mail, I became angry, hurt, and disheartened. In my mind, I saw myself as giving more to this church than the church had asked. Now, the church was dealing with me in what I perceived to be an unfair and impersonal way. I called the chair of the committee. He assured me that from the committee's perspective this was a minor policy issue, and he apologized for any hurt it had caused me.

However, I couldn't let this go. In my mind, I built this into an issue of the church's ingratitude. I felt that I was giving this church the best of myself, and the committee had acted without asking for my input. My anger and hurt went on for several days. In talking with my wife, who is much calmer than I, I recognized how disproportionate my response was to the issue. I felt rejected even when I knew this hadn't been the intention of the committee. The chair even apologized and offered to rectify the situation. After good input from Diane, I finally settled down, but it cost me a headache and a good night's sleep.

You would think by now I could handle this kind of situation better. Intellectually, I knew what was going on with me. I've always had a tendency to take perceived slights and expand them into "They don't appreciate me. They take me for granted. They aren't being fair." While at one level I realize the destructive pattern, I've struggled with this emotionally throughout my ministry.

I've heard people talk about the irrationality of such thinking. I've read articles about what this kind of anger does to us physically. I've preached sermons about migrating church members who get their feelings hurt and who hop to the next church. Yet, when my feelings are hurt, I respond in much the same way.

As critical as I may be about the destructive grooves churches develop or ecclesiastical systems that seem to have lost their reason for being, I'm wired much the same way. Why is that? There's usually some reason even for the bad patterns we develop and continue. I did get attention. My wife felt badly for me, and while Diane didn't think it was the major issue I saw it to be, she did empathize with me because I felt badly. The chair of the committee at church and several members called me and apologized for any hurt they had caused me and reassured me how needed I was at the church. That felt good.

Was my anger out of proportion? Yes! Was it worth the headache and the bad night of sleep? No! Am I proud of my behavior? No! Did it feel good to have people tell me they were sorry they may have offended me and that I was needed at the church? Yes! Would I do it that way again? I would like to say no. I would like to tell you about my willingness to change and not to let things like this disturb me so much. Then I would like to tell you that never again will I use something like this to get attention and affirmation.

I guess we'll have to wait to see if a similar situation arises. I don't like to pout. I don't like to manipulate a situation in order to squeeze praise from others to soothe my personal injury. I expect better from myself. However, I know how difficult it is for me to break unhealthy patterns. I guess this difficulty in changing myself has helped me to understand better how enormously difficult it is for a church to change the way it reacts and responds to challenges. No matter how capable you and I may consider our-selves as preachers, no matter how clearly we may believe we have articulated the vision, the fact is that some of the ways the church behaves will be that way throughout our ministries and long after we have gone.

A second element that helps pastors understand that not everybody and everything will change is that the church is an institution with traditions and structures (usually buildings and property), and that all of these things become important to many of the people. As pastors, we become a part of that institution. I have never been pastor of a church in which raising the budget hasn't been important.

How do we react to the church as an institution? In one sense, those of us who are preachers need to stand against the idea of the church as institu-tion. Obviously, the fundamental danger of any institution is that it exists for its own self-preservation. When we read the New Testament, for example, we see that faith began in an experience and encounter with Jesus Christ. To Jesus, knowing him and following him seem to be the primary components of faith. Jesus himself seems to have little interest in creating an institution that bears his name. Jesus was on the move. His ministry was mobile, and he preached, taught, and healed wherever he met people. The idea that pro-pelled Jesus' ministry was to go to where people were. He didn't preach at certain times of the week or conduct a mid-week Bible study in the chapel of some church where he was the senior pastor.

However, after Jesus' resurrection, the church began to show signs of institutionalism. Some of Paul's letters are addressed to bishops, elders, and other leaders of various churches. After the New Testament, evidence indi-cates that institutionalism grew stronger as churches became more structured and more organized.

Is institutionalism bad? It can be if the organization becomes more important than the experience of people with the God who cares for them. That's why one of the tasks of pastoral preaching is to remind people that behind the structure there is the life-changing story of a God invested in humankind. If we lose touch with that story, we are in the deepest trouble. If keeping the nose of the institution above the waterline becomes the pastor's chief objective, then we have lost sight of our reason for being. In the edifice of the institution called church, we are called to speak about the story of God who breaks into human history and calls us to experience transcen-dence. Edifice is the *means* to the end of our experience and encounter with

God. If edifice becomes the *end*, then institutionalism has trumped incarnation.

However, institutions are not inherently evil. In fact, they are an inevitable part of life. If experience, thought important, is all there is, then we move around with our own version of the story, and community never happens. Jesus encouraged the need for "koinonia" and "ecclesia." Partnership in the gospel and togetherness as the body of Christ are essential themes in Pauline theology. The church developed because people needed to worship together, to work together, and to have their experiences develop into a faith that put words to the spiritual encounters people had. From the New Testament, it's obvious that the church tried to find a unifying way through the myriad interpretations some people had of their experiences with Jesus Christ. The church, in effect, became the guardian of faith and the guide for people to understand the traditions that became important.

Obviously, the church through its history hasn't always done the most exemplary job of both guarding and guiding people in the faith. The Crusades are a sad chapter in the history of the Christian faith. Before that, Emperor Constantine after his conversion "compelled" people to come to his Christian faith. Today, in the church of Jesus Christ, we have those who seem to possess parts of the faith as their own, and necessary humility is lost.

With this said, however, the church, as imperfect as it may be, is the place where pastors are called to preach and to serve. What if ministers could see the possibilities of a church instead of just its problems? Why don't churches change as quickly as some of us ministers would like? Does the bureaucracy of the church sometimes make any change seem like an interminable process? That's part of it! Is it the reluctance of some irascible folks who will vote against whatever it is? That's part of it. Some people are threatened by the slightest change, and as ministers we will live our lives with folks who remind us of the good old days when hell was hell, heaven was heaven, the Bible says it and we believe it.

Yet, there may be something more positive that we clergy can celebrate rather than condemn. Whatever its failings are, the church is the group of people that led most of us to faith. It's the place where we learned the stories, the songs, and words like grace and love that are part of our spiritual bloodstream. Granted, I didn't learn the historical critical approach to biblical studies at church. Was I ever surprised when I went to college and learned, for instance, about J, E, D, and P, which are abbreviations for the supposed four different streams that flow through the first five books of the Old

Testament? No Sunday school teacher ever mentioned that. But after my initial reaction of arrogance and anger, I came to realize what a tremendous gift of time and energy these people in my church had given to me. I had to reshape some of my ideas, but I was grateful for those folks who had loved me enough to share a faith that I could shape.

So much preaching and ministry depends upon how we see the church. Some churches are dysfunctional and even pathologically sick, just as some people and family systems are. Even healthy churches have their mixture of good and bad, but so do we as ministers. How do we see the church? Do we view the church as bad children who need scolding? Do we look at only the parts of the church that aren't what we want them to be? Or are we grateful for those who care deeply, who love God the best they can, and who genuinely want to be more of what they have been called to be?

I wish I had begun the journey as a pastor with more gratitude for the church. When our son, David, was so ill, our family was thrust into the world of neurosurgery. Fortunately, Diane is a nurse, so she could help me understand better this world of new words. Some of the doctors were callous in their bedside manner. They spewed out medical terms that meant nothing to me. At times, I felt incredibly stupid because I believed the physicians thought I should know these things.

Other neurosurgeons were far more compassionate. I know they had to maintain their professional distance. I know they had strenuous demands. However, they would sit down, explain the situation in words I could understand, and most of all I felt that our family was important to them and that they cared about us. How important that was. We wanted to make the right decisions. Our family was crushed by this unexpected event. It was so important to know that the physicians had not only the knowledge but also the care for us.

Those of us with theological training are fortunate. We have been able to focus on what for many of us is the most important aspect of life. We have accumulated information. Now we go to the church to try to share that information, to help inspire people to live more faithfully to God, to comfort those for whom the shadows are dark and deep, and to challenge the church to see that we are all people on a mission. In a figurative sense, we pull up the chair in the room and speak in words and tones that communicate that we do care for these people. Perhaps, like even the most skilled neurosurgeon, we can't always "fix" everything. We will never make everything the way we may want it to be. The church will have its blemishes and jagged edges. So do we. We speak to people not as if they are spiritually inferior or benighted because they don't know all the words and concepts we've learned at seminary. We preach to them with the kind of compassion we all need. In the final analysis, this may be the best means to change any of us.

HAVING COURAGE
TO CHANGE OURSELVES

Those of us who are ministers often see ourselves as catalysts for changes in others. I've heard seminary and divinity school professors admonish students to be prophetic. Sometimes, these professors haven't had much experience in churches themselves, and they turn loose boiling cauldrons who wind up having to find another church in six months. The church doesn't change because it feels assaulted. The only thing that changes is the address of the pastor and the resolution of the church next time to get a minister from a different seminary.

This isn't intended to diminish the importance of the prophetic elements in preaching. Amos burst into the center of power and used words like "cows" to describe some of the women who lived too well while many of the people had little or nothing. Some of us who are pastors would like to be as brazen and bold as the shepherd from Tekoa. Whatever our personal style, however, we are called to address issues like injustice and inequality. Part of our preaching is intended to provide ways in which the Spirit of God can effect needed changes in all of our lives.

What about changes in the lives of those of us who preach? In a profound way, our own willingness to change provides a model for the church. Rigidity projected from the pulpit is hardly a healthful attribute when we call people to continuing conversion.

Those of us who go to be the pastor of a church soon learn that we all have places of strength but also places where we need to grow. Several times I've alluded to the fact that I have not been very good at monitoring my own energy level and my own use of time. Taking a meaningful Sabbath time has been extremely difficult. Even when I sit down to watch the news or a sporting event on television, I'm usually reading a newspaper or magazine at the same time. In my life, doing has taken priority over being. I'm good at working, organizing, setting goals, and managing my time, but I'm very bad at relaxing, playing, and enjoying myself.

This approach to life directly affects my preaching. Most of my sermons are designed to challenge the church to do more and to become more. Sabbath time is seldom a subject of my sermons. This desire to move people along also reflecta itself in my style. I use words like "passion" and "energy" to describe my interaction with the congregation.

The problem isn't that I was entirely wrong in my view of the preaching task. I was half-right, and sometimes that can be more dangerous than being all wrong. When you and I are partially right, we can develop a strong case to defend our position. After all, most churches do need to be more involved in becoming the people of God on mission. I could cite Jesus who asked folks to follow him and to take up their crosses daily.

What I ignored was the significance of Jesus' Sabbath moments. There are ample indications that our Lord needed time away for quiet prayer and even naps. While Jesus didn't have much success at resting, he did want to escape the constant demands on his time and energy. Jesus knew how imperative it was in his life to spend those moments "alone with the Alone."

In the past few years of my life, I've attempted to schedule those times of Sabbath. For so long, I thought the pastor should be available and always on call. I dreaded when the telephone rang at night. I could feel the tension throughout my body. While I'm still working on this reflective side, I am trying to give myself permission to "be still and know God is . . . ."

How I wish I had done this earlier in my ministry. I would have been a better person. I probably wouldn't have been so tired and so on edge at times. I could have approached my ministry with more enjoyment. As it was, every morning signaled a new day in which I felt I had to go out to prove myself all over again.

If I had established a better rhythm between rest and work, I also could have set a better example for others who lived their lives the way I lived mine. I think of marriages that ended because one or both of the partners had no time to care for the relationship. I remember children who were pushed into excessive activities because they were the progeny of "hurried parents." While I preached sermons about the need for prayer, silence, meditation, reflection, and relaxation, I never let those messages come home to roost in my life. I was the "hurried pastor," and at times I wonder if I had any idea about what I was racing to achieve.

It is important for pastors and ministers to check not only what we do but also why we do it. What motivates us? What drives us? What voices tell us that speaking is better than silence, that actions are better than reflection, and that doing, achieving, and accomplishing are the ways to lead a fulfilled life?

Each year my family doctor gives me a physical examination. He asks me the same questions: "Any changes since last year? Are you exercising? What about your eating and sleeping? Are you drinking plenty of water?" Then he checks me over, does blood work, and lets me know how I'm doing. So far, so good! My doctor knows me well enough to know that I overschedule myself. "Why?" he asks. "I don't know," I reply. But the fact is I do know. Deep down, I struggle with trying to prove myself. I want to know that I have value. As a child, I learned my lesson too well. Achieve and you will be rewarded. What I didn't realize is that this approach to life carries an expensive price tag. I've looked at too few full moons, not enough beautiful flowers; I haven't sat and talked with someone I love nearly enough; I haven't enjoyed enough vacations. If God thought it wise to take a Sabbath, then it's about time I learned from God.

If we think of life as a journey, then those of us who minister are not only exegetes of the lives of others, but we are also examining ourselves and asking, "What keeps us from knowing the fullness of our faith?" Then, by the grace of God, we confess those things and pray for strength to be more whole. We want that for ourselves as well as for those who listen to our words and to the way we live.

Beyond personal growth, there is also our professional development. With regard to preaching, this is particularly important. Our task as preachers is not simply to say something but to try to get the message heard. Probably no area of life has changed more in the last twenty-five years than information communication. The next few years will see even more advances. One of the ramifications of these changes is that those who try to communicate need to be extremely alert to shifts in the way people receive information. The preaching style of 2002 may not be suited to 2012. What worked effectively in an American society where Christianity was the normative faith may not work so well in a highly pluralistic culture where religious and ethnic demographics shift rapidly.

Let me point to several issues. First, we as preachers are going to have to reexamine what we assume our listeners know. We can't always make cursory allusions to biblical stories that may be an intricate part of the fabric of our faith. Abraham may be unknown to some. Some of our listeners may have never heard of Sarah. When I prepare a sermon, I try to take figuratively someone who has little knowledge of the Bible into my study so that I can ask occasionally, "Would this person have any idea what I'm saying?" This has caused me to try to eliminate statements in the sermon such as "We should be like Abraham and Sarah." While we should be like Sarah and Abraham, the issue for the preaching minister is, "Do people know what I'm talking about?" Unfortunately, surveys indicate that people may believe the Bible, but many of them have little knowledge of words or stories we preachers use. This doesn't mean that we stop using the stories or even the great words of our faith. However, it does mean that we need to linger a little longer and allow everyone to experience the "thickness" of these words and narratives.

A second area that we need to examine again is how people's lives are changed. That is, how do we most effectively preach in a transformative way? Many of us grew up on a steady diet of propositional and argumentative preaching. The preacher stated the thesis and then gave points in the sermon designed either to explain or to prove that the basic idea of the sermon was true. The primary target area for listeners was the mind. The preacher's rationale was "If I can prove my point, then I will change people's minds, and these people will be transformed."

I'm not opting for "mindless" preaching. All good sermons have a certain organizing principle and an appeal that speaks to the minds of listeners. At the same time, we realize that we don't live by "head" alone. Most of us live also with our hearts. We are people with emotions, and sometimes we are most damaged at the emotive level of our lives. In fact, at the risk of overstating, I believe that a person who approaches faith only as an intellectual exercise may be trying to avoid a holistic faith that touches us at each level of our existence.

Transformative preaching is more than trying to get people to swap one idea for another. Rather, transformative preaching rises from the prayer that the Spirit of God will use our words to effect change in each of us. This kind of preaching also takes seriously that incarnation has been God's supreme way to connect with us. Therefore, we speak in ways that reflect the incarnational experience for our time. We speak visually, imaginatively, and pictorially. We tell stories not to give listeners a few minutes' relief from a cascade of ideas, but to show that God comes in the flow of a story. Most people understand their lives in terms of stories.

This doesn't mean that every sermon has to be an extended narrative. Neither does it mean that effective preaching is a parade of stories, none of which seem to relate to the others or to a unifying focus for the sermon. Ideas are still important, but preaching needs to ask, "How is that idea incarnated?" Can I give people something that they can see as well as hear?

The author John Updike was asked the secret of a great writing. Updike replied, "Pay attention." Life unravels in front of us and around us in personal and pictorial ways. In the Gospel of John there is concern about a profound idea. The idea is "Logos." The "Logos" or Word became flesh and dwelt among us. This is not a good idea that we decide only in our minds to accept or reject. This is someone we see. The great idea of God becomes flesh and blood, and we experience him with all of our senses and all of ourselves.

A final area that I believe will become even more important in preaching is the creation of intimacy between preacher and hearer. Again, the incarnation is the theological pattern. As Christians, we believe that God's ultimate revelation was being with us. That is threatening. Some ministers choose to construct great distance between themselves and the congregation. The preaching event is highly formal; the language of the sermon is stilted; the minister stands behind a formidable-looking podium; and the sermon is read as if getting each word on paper in proper sequence is the primary objective of preaching. There is little if any eye contact; limited use of the body of the preacher to reinforce the words; and an absence of stories that may disclose the preacher as a person with feelings and experiences of both joy and pain.

I share these things realizing that we can abuse any or all of them. Not using a manuscript does not mean little if any preparation. In fact, it means a different kind of preparation that may involve more time. The use of our bodies doesn't mean prancing from one end of the pulpit area to the other. People get tired when the movement of the preacher isn't focused and congruent with the message. Self-disclosure doesn't mean emotional exhibitionism. The aim of Christian preaching is to lift up Jesus Christ, and if that doesn't happen, then we have not preached. The means of preaching must never overshadow the end of preaching. Whatever techniques, strategies, methods, or means we use in preaching, the final test is whether we have shared God.

The Message We Preach

In this final chapter and the appendix, I want to try to do a couple of things. In this chapter, I want to talk about establishing a pattern or rhythm for sermon preparation and delivery. In the appendix, I want to introduce you to sermons that illustrate pastoral preaching. For that section, each of my fellow ministers wrote a brief account that helps us understand the factors that fashioned their messages. Current or former students of mine have preached some of these sermons. Two are women: Ray Beale and Rhonda Van Dyke Colby. Both are in the Baptist Theological Seminary at Richmond's Doctor of Ministry program. I have had them in class and grown to appreciate them as friends and fellow ministers. I've also asked Dr. Phillip Reynolds to contribute a funeral message. Phillip is a graduate of our Doctor of Ministry program and is a caring and competent pastor. One sermon is from the young man who has been my student assistant for two years. Stephen Cook is like a son to me. When I listen to him preach and watch him minister to people, I feel so good about the future of the church.

Several of the sermons are ones that I have preached. I'm not accustomed to writing my sermons, so I'm writing them as I best remember how they were spoken. In the sermons from others and my own sermons, I've asked people to retain as much of the oral quality as possible. These aren't well-documented term papers complete with footnotes; they are sermons designed to be heard.

ESTABLISHING A PATTERN FOR SERMON PREPARATION AND DELIVERY

A pastor quickly learns the importance of establishing a rhythm and a plan for ministry and a schedule for the demands of preaching. Sometimes an unexpected event or crisis interrupts that schedule, but as ministers, we create unnecessary stress for ourselves if we have to reinvent the wheel of our scheduling every week. When it comes to preparing a sermon, each minister develops a personal pattern. It is essential that we have a pattern and limit ourselves on each part of the preparation process, allowing ourselves enough time to develop the message and to know it well enough when we share it with our listeners.

Probably the greatest danger, besides little if any preparation for the message, is the pastor who takes too much time with one aspect of preparation and doesn't allow enough time for the whole process. A good example is the exegetical work that we do on a biblical text. As students, we are taught to research a passage of Scripture thoroughly, but the fact is that if we preach on the Gospel of John, we don't have time to look at every commentary. We need to stay acquainted with the seminal commentaries and then learn to live with the sense that we always could do more if time constraints weren't a factor. I'd like to offer the way I prepare a sermon, recognizing that each minister will change, modify, or ignore this according to that minister's style and situation. My concern is that we have a way to do our sermons. We may alter the process a bit throughout our ministry, but we waste too much time when we begin each week by asking, "Now, what is it that I do first?"

Selection of the Biblical Text

I usually take a day or two by myself to plan my preaching about six months in advance. It's important for me to get the text, select a tentative title, and then write one or two sentences about why that text is important or what I may want to say about that passage. I use several methods to select the passages. I usually look at the lectionary readings. While the lectionary is a relatively new help for those of us in some of the free church traditions, it has been a valuable preaching tool for centuries.

The lectionary helps us understand the flow of the Christian Year. Advent becomes even more meaningful as we understand that the coming of Christ is emphasized as a personal experience, a past coming of the Messiah, and the anticipation of the second inbreak of God into human history.

When I use the lectionary, I select one of the four texts offered. One of my concerns in a sermon is to interlace the biblical text with contemporary life. I find this much easier to do with one text.

While I appreciate the lectionary, I don't follow it slavishly. Sometimes I do a series of not more than six sermons on a challenge or need that the congregation faces. Always, my plan for preaching is subject to change. Perhaps something happens in our community or our world, and almost everybody's mind is on it. If we don't speak to that issue on Sunday, we miss a "preachable moment."

Once I select my biblical texts for the six months, I make a folder for each sermon and put into the folder anything I read, see, or hear that may be useful. Also, I give the basic information about the sermon to the other ministers involved in planning the worship service so we can discuss, clarify, or alter the direction I've chosen for the message.

Reading the Biblical Text

This is probably the most transformative change I've made in my sermon preparation. Largely inspired by Paul Ricouer and Fred Craddock, the first move I make in preparing a sermon is to read a biblical text. I read it silently and then aloud. I read it slowly, looking for people, words, phrases, or anything that draws my attention. I jot random thoughts. After reading the text several times, I look at what I've written and see if anything stands out as a possible focus or thematic statement for the sermon. All of this is done with only the biblical word, perhaps in several translations or in the Greek or Hebrew if I feel confident enough. Frankly, my skills in the original biblical languages are such that I have to rely on my aids to help me understand the meanings and nuances of the words.

Reading the biblical text this way often becomes a profound personal encounter. In a sense, I'm trying to internalize the passage and come to a fairly clear idea of what I want to say in the sermon. The danger with this part of preparation occurs when we as ministers, in our search for the new idea or focus that will leave the congregation gasping at a new insight, cannot settle on what we want to say. One of the difficult aspects of preaching is living with the discomfort that we may not have found the "crown jewel." Since the preparation process involves different movements, the secret is not to become frozen at one particular point in the process. Creative preachers want to say things in a way that have never been said before. We'd like to think even Jesus would sit up and listen to us because of our insights.

Trying to do that impossible task every Sunday will find us on Saturday night still wondering, "Now, what is it that I want to say?"

Checking the Resources

After we have an idea of what we want to say about a biblical text, we approach commentaries, dictionaries, and other helps. Reading these resources helps focus our study on the theme of our sermon.

Once in awhile, we may change our message simply because there's no way the text will support our focus. However, I've found that many of my students come up with superb ideas that may not be found in any commentary. I encourage them to trust their instincts. I know there is a fine balance between legitimate curiosity and preaching that flies off into our own sermonic solar system, but, frankly, I want to encourage students to trust themselves as interpreters of the Bible.

It's also important that we set time limits for this part of sermon preparation. Like you, I was educated in writing term papers. Usually, the more books we had in the bibliography, the better. We were encouraged to look at everything we could find on the subject. The preparation of a weekly sermon is different. We don't have time. We will probably feel guilty because we hear the faint voice of our favorite seminary professor who admonished us to research diligently. As preachers, though, we probably need to select two or three seminal commentaries on our text, read them, put them back on our bookshelves, and be ready for the next step.

Structuring the Sermon

After hearing a sermon, have you ever said, "I know there was a good idea in that sermon, but I never understood how the pastor was trying to develop it"? That's a good indication of a preacher who is creative in developing a point for the sermon but doesn't leave enough time to develop the organization of the message.

Let's begin by acknowledging that organization is important. Reacting negatively to propositional sermons with proverbial points and a poem, some preachers have responded with a free-flowing, stream of consciousness preaching. Good ideas may be expressed, but there is no organizing whole or logical movement to the sermon. People find it difficult to listen because if they check out mentally for even a moment, they have no idea where to reboard the train. The introduction of new forms to proclamation is not an invitation to a lack of cohesion in the sermon. Sermons still need to start somewhere, go someplace, and hopefully end sometime and in a place that fits the movement of the message. Most of us like surprises, but we also like to know that sermons, like life, have some direction. Congregations can enjoy a variety of sermon designs as long as they are confident in their pastors' organization, and know that whatever sermons pastors deliver will have design and direction. However, congregations have difficulty with chaotic messages that move all over the board. As listeners, we are dropped into the middle of the pool, forced to tread water until we're exhausted, and then have to make our own way to the side of the pool. Such sermons are usually marked by too many things the preacher tries to say, by unclear transitions, and by stories or other illustrations that seem to have no connection to each other.

With regard to specific designs or patterns a preacher uses, the possibilities are virtually endless. We as ministers need to find forms that are congenial to our own gifts, that will best communicate the message to our listeners, and that take seriously the form of the biblical text we use.

One of the most popular designs these days is the narrative or story sermon. Eugene Lowry is probably the homiletician most associated with story preaching, although it's interesting that many ministers in the black tradition intuited the power of stories well before white homileticians thought they discovered this "new land." Lowry proposes a "plotted" approach to the sermon: create tension at the beginning of the message; exacerbate that tension; give clues to resolution; and end the sermon by offering what you consider the fundamental resolution to the tension.

Without trying to talk about all the dimensions of narrative preaching— because there are a multitude of ways in which the term is used—let me say a strong word in favor of stories. This is the way much of the Bible comes to us. For example, Genesis starts, "In the beginning God . . . ." What we don't have is a philosophical/theological discussion on the nature of God. What we do have is a God who works within the stories of people and who reveals who God is through the events in people's lives. We also know that most of us tell about our lives in narrative terms. We begin to know ourselves, and we allow others to know us, as we tell the stories that have shaped us. Most of us don't interpret our lives as a procession of propositions. Our lives include places and people who have nurtured us, loved us. or maybe rejected and abused us.

Narrative preaching takes seriously both the Bible and individuals. We ministers begin to develop a personal style and then try to make the changes that will help us communicate more effectively. I have developed a style that is comfortable to my way of processing life but hopefully includes elements that speak to those whose patterns of thinking differ from mine. Regardless, we have to understand that we can't emulate every preacher we enjoy, and we will live in a constant state of frustration if we want to preach just like Fred Craddock, Barbara Brown Taylor, Tom Long, Gardner Taylor, or whomever we admire. We learn things from these people. For example, Barbara Brown Taylor is the consummate crafter of words. Her preaching is like poetry. I learn from her sermons. However, I can't be Barbara Brown Taylor any more than I can be Fred Craddock. So, even as we learn from others, we should develop styles of preaching consistent with our personalities and gifts. For example, several things have become increasingly important in the formation of my sermons.

First, I spend much more time these days trying to retell the text I'm using. I attempt to do this with imagination and a sense of wonder about what God is doing. Many folks no longer have even the most basic information about the Bible. Reading the text and jumping immediately to what we believe it says prevents all of us from experiencing and hopefully enjoying the Bible.

Second, I want to have organization to the sermon. When I come to the point of trying to visualize the message, organization helps me avoid the manuscript or copious notes. Much of the time, I take my organizing principle from the text. Since texts have movements with messages instead of outlines with points, I try to keep this sense of movement in the sermon, emphasizing places that contribute to the main focus or point of the sermon. Unlike in traditional expository preaching, I try to expose "something" of what the biblical passage says, but don't feel the necessity of commenting on everything in the verses. Early in the sermon, I give some implicit or explicit word about the direction in which I'm going with the message.

Two things in particular are important to me in the development of the sermon. I like to weave the biblical text throughout the sermon and then connect it to present-day life. I like to speak of the biblical passage in the present tense. I'm attempting to collapse some of the distance between the ancient word and our world. I avoid sermon structures in which the text is first exegeted and then applied. I want to suggest that the text has interest and relevancy for the listeners, and that the biblical text carries its own relevance for our lives.

A second thing I do is to weave comments, propositions, and stories throughout the sermon. While I have done purely "story" sermons, I believe that when we speak to groups of people, we have to recognize divergent listening styles. People listen to both ideas and images. If I want a certain idea to be part of the sermon, I immediately ask, "How can I image that? How can I put flesh on ideas so the sermon doesn't become just an appeal to the mind?" At the same time, I don't want to tell stories that have no organizing principle. When I tell stories that lack organization, I find that my motivation is to entertain or to get people to listen. It usually becomes "preaching light."

I want stories or illustrations to contribute to the movement of the message. That makes it much easier for me to "see" the sermon and to preach it without an overreliance on notes.

Visualizing the Message

As many ministers do, I have changed my method of preparation over the years. Initially, I wrote a manuscript and then attempted to memorize it. While memorizing is a good method if we want precise words and phrases, it usually worked to my disadvantage. First, my main concern on Sunday morning was to say the right words in the right sequence. Though I made eye contact with the listeners, I devoted my energy to getting the words right. I wasn't able to pay attention to the subtle and sometimes not-so-subtle ways listeners gave feedback. The primary transaction of the sermon was between the notes on the pulpit and me. Those were my two main concerns. The people in the congregation were a distant third, even though I would have told you that I had prepared the message hoping they would hear.

Trying to memorize the sermon also created problems for me in the absorption and delivery of the message. While I tried to keep a holistic view of the sermon, I often saw it as a series of phrases that I memorized and delivered in a choppy, episodic way. I didn't realize this until I listened to tapes of some of my sermons and saw that at times I preached a sequence of sentences rather than a whole sermon. My breathing and my voice inflection rose and fell with the passing of one sentence and the beginning of the next. Again, each minister needs to develop patterns for structuring sermons that are congenial to personal gifts. However, I am concerned that since much of our education as pastors is script-oriented, we need to work harder to develop oral skills. For me, this was the problem. I was writing sentences in the sermon that fit better in a college term paper. The sentences were too long; some of the words were too ponderous for the ear; and for me, the primary motive to change my method of preparation was that I didn't enjoy or find fulfillment in the whole sermon process.

Over the years, I've developed a pattern in which I write out one 8-x-11-inch sheet of paper with the movement of the sermon. I try to finish this by Tuesday. On Friday and Saturdays, I go back to see what I've written and try to visualize the flow of the sermon. I may add or subtract a story or an illustration. I think about the movement of the sermon. Does it start at a place where people are and does it move in a logical way to the place where I want the hearers and me to go? What about the transitions? Are they smooth, and will they help people to move with me through the sermon? I look at the stories and illustrations. Do they fit? Can I tell them concisely? Do I believe that what I'm saying can make a difference to all of us? Am I seeing this message as an offering to God, or are parts of it—particular self-disclosure or humor—really there to draw attention to me? When I enter the pulpit on Sunday, I take at most a 3-x-5-inch card on which I've listed the primary transitions of the sermon. I try to internalize and visualize the message so that I don't rely on the card, and so that I can help the listeners re-experience with me the joy, the comfort, the challenge, or whatever I've experienced in the preparation of the message.

Again, I want to emphasize that preaching without a manuscript doesn't make a sermon better or a preacher more "spiritual." Some of our faith traditions have been heavily influenced by revivalism. With its emphasis on the work of the Holy Spirit, a sentiment developed among some people influenced by revivalism that the preacher should go to the pulpit and let the Spirit lead. Unfortunately, the Holy Spirit gets blamed for a lot of aimless sermons. If the Holy Spirit works in the sanctuary, then God can also work in the pastor's study.

Not writing a manuscript for the sermon doesn't mean taking preparation for the preaching event any less seriously. In fact, it takes me about the same amount of time to prepare to preach. However, I prepare differently. I spend more time imagining the movement of the sermon and envisioning what kind of impact I hope the message will have. Rather than memorizing phrases, I visualize the various parts of the sermon and think about what in the message may cause me to stop to examine my own life. In my preparation, I may pause to ponder why something touches me, and this may lead me to pause briefly at those points when I preach. All of us have heard preachers who know how to use pauses effectively. The sermon is not a cease-less stream of words. Preachers react to their own words, and often those words are spoken for us as much as for those who sit in the congregation.

This may lead preachers to say some things in a hesitant, almost fearful way. But aren't our most powerful words said with some hesitancy? When I tell somebody I love her or care for him, I think about what that means. It's a commitment. What happens to somebody else makes a difference to me. Think about what you and I as ministers say in our messages. We talk about the most crucial things in life. We speak about God's love for us and our love for God. We remind others and ourselves of what God wants to do for us and what God wants us to do for God.

Paul Scherer, a great preacher of another generation, coined the term "spiritual speakeasies." After preaching for a while, most of us can get on our feet and say words. We strive to keep our wonder, our awe, our astonishment that God can take our words and use them as a means to transform us. As I visualize and imagine the unfolding of the sermon, I want to think not only about the flow of words, the transitions, and the stories, but about the God who works through our often fumbling and feeble words.

However you and I choose to prepare ourselves to preach, the essential fact is that we do prepare ourselves and our message. None of us who try to take proclamation seriously ever feel we have done all we can to get ready for that sacred moment. We face time constrictions and demands on our energy, and we know as pastors that we are pilgrims still on the road. We haven't reached the eternal city. We "see through a glass darkly." There is so much of the mystery of God to know and to experience. Yet, with all of these factors, we know that some people will be waiting for us at the church house on Sunday morning. They will be waiting for us to say something. What an unbelievable opportunity for preachers. We don't have the last word, but we want to share words that we have prayed about, thought about, and cared about. Our hope is that in the message we have taken seriously, the message of God will be heard. Stranger things have happened. We take the pulpit seriously. We speak the words, the images, and the stories that have been born in us, and we pray that in the holy hour of worship, they will be born from above.

Speaking the Message

The delivery or release of the sermon is integrally related to the preparation of the sermon. When this isn't the case, difficulties arise. For example, some people see the preparation and the proclamation of the message as two distinct events. The minister works in his or her study and finally arrives at a carefully constructed sermon. At this time, preparation for delivery begins. The minister goes back through the manuscript or notes time after time, trying to memorize or internalize the sequence of words. The process of preparation and actual preaching are separated.

When we separate preparation and preaching, we fail to take seriously that speaking the sermon is not just one movement in the sermon event; it's the culmination of all that we as preachers do. From the outset of preparation, we want to remember that everything we do as preachers moves toward the moment of proclamation. This shapes our focus. For example, as exciting as the background study of a biblical text may be for some, we don't want to spend all of our time trying to understand the historical intentionality of a text and the nuances of every Hebrew or Greek word. This is difficult when we have to unload the guilt from every seminary professor who told us that his or her area was the most critical. I had a New Testament professor who was absolutely passionate about his discipline. I'm glad. This professor helped me see how his library of twenty-seven books was fresh with history, narrative, poetry, and hymns and how all of those forms resonated with aliveness. For this teacher, the New Testament wasn't a portion of Scripture that needed to be made relevant. It was for him as relevant as the front page of the *New York Times*.

However, this professor wasn't preaching a new sermon every Sunday. Neither was he doing funerals or weddings. He didn't have staff meetings or as many counseling sessions or committee meetings as most pastors do. When I left the seminary as a student, I thanked this teacher for what he had meant to me. At the same time, I thought to myself, "If he ever shows up unexpectedly to hear me preach, he may be disappointed." In medical terms, this professor was a specialist. As a pastor, I was a general practitioner.

Thus, those of us as pastors have to keep moving in our sermon preparation with an eye on the moment of speaking. This focus will affect the words we use in the sermon. Words should be concise. Sentences should be tight. Images and illustrations should be succinct and fit the context. If we use an idea that requires lengthy explanation, we probably should save that for a time when we are teaching. The sermon arrives at the listener's ear. Therefore, we should prepare the message with the idea that people hear our words, images, and stories one time. Because we as ministers spend far more time with the sermon, we need to resist the notion that everybody has the same investment and awareness of the message that we have. We need to remind ourselves, "The people will hear my words one time. Are what I'm saying and the way I'm saying it clear enough to be heard and received?"

When we speak the sermon, we also want to keep in mind several important factors. First, we should strive for authenticity and sincerity in our preaching. This isn't a contrived authenticity. From the beginning of our preparation, we should strive not only to bear the words but also to hear the words. As Elijah, we should try to sit where the people sit. What does the message say to me? Is it important? Can it make a difference in my life if I truly hear it? What we don't want to do as ministers is to prepare a message and then in the final stages try to claim its importance and make it real for us.

Most listeners can detect whether the words the minister speaks are real to her or his life or whether the message remains in the far country. There is a difference between the professed love of two people who share nothing but pictures and long-distance correspondence and the romance of two people who spend time together talking about matters of the heart and the head. At the risk of sounding silly, the good preacher romances and is romanced by the biblical text so that what emerges in the sermon sounds like a love affair and not the musings of a minister too distant from the text and too distant from the listeners.

This does not mean that for ministers to achieve authenticity, we need to pretend that we have understood or appropriated all the truths in the Bible. If preaching is a romantic affair with the text, then we always want to preserve the mystery of love. Neither do we want to preach from the Bible as if we possess it. In a relationship of love, a person doesn't possess the beloved. That's insecurity. That's jealousy. We may call it love, but real love sets the beloved free to become all she or he can be.

Neither do ministers preach as if we possess the Bible. The Bible speaks of things that will always be beyond us. It calls us to a selfless life that few ever live to the fullest. In the Bible, writers refer to God as Spirit and Love, neither of which can be captured even by the most eloquent preacher. Good preachers always reach beyond themselves and point to the inbreaking reign of God both in their lives and the lives of others. Perhaps this is part of what the Apostle Paul meant when he warned not to preach ourselves but to preach Jesus Christ. When we preach only what we have experienced and only what we are living, we dangerously limit the God whose goodness far exceeds our goodness. Authentic preaching stretches us. It speaks of the God who is with us, but it also speaks of the God ahead of us who calls us to possibilities beyond our boldest imagination.

In this sense, the authentic minister speaks the deepest truth. There is truth that holds us and keeps us moving through the darkest valleys. There is truth we hold in our minds and hearts that becomes the values for our living. But try as we may, the God of all truth refuses to be tamed and domesticated. We, as preachers, point to the horizon and call the church to move by faith into those places and spaces of life where God leads, and all we can do is drop our nets and follow only God knows where.

Preaching needs to be authentic. As we share our sermons, we should remember that many people today are looking for their minister to speak as a spiritual companion. In my opinion, the days of the great pulpit orators are over. By pulpit orators, I mean preachers of another era who were known for the way they mounted the pulpit, for the way they spoke as if they had breakfast with God each morning, and for the intonation, inflection, grandiose gestures, and booming voices that made listeners say, "This is a real preacher!"

By no means do I want to create the image of a new kind of minister who comes to the pulpit as if this is the last place he or she wants to be. Communicative skills are important. How we use our voices, our bodies, our hands, our feet—all of ourselves—is vital to effective communication. Frankly, I am concerned that in some religious circles, preaching has grown too timid. We don't trust our words, and so the worship service becomes a cascade of film clips, audio-visual effects, dialogue, and a thousand other things we use to avoid one person speaking a message in love to other people.

I believe passionately in preaching and in what it can be as a transformative instrument to turn all of us more in the direction of the Divine. However, I also believe that our fundamental images of ourselves as preachers are undergoing a seismic shift. Instead of striving to be rulers of the pulpit or desiring to emulate some great orator of another generation, we want to speak as guides and companions of people on the quest to know God and to be known more by God.

This is a more relational style of communication. Obviously, we have to modify the style to fit the place where we speak and the number of people who listen. However, the object isn't for listeners to leave the worship service shaking their heads at the personal magnetism of the preacher but to be more aware of the God for whom people seem to hunger and thirst these days. Some ministers do have personal charisma. By virtue of their gifts as people and their development as preachers, these ministers will draw attention. However, we need to be careful not to fall into the trap of being deluded by people who may feed minister's egos. We begin to think too highly of ourselves and too little of the God who has blessed us and calls us to bless others.

Sometimes I think about what I want people to remember about me as a preacher. I am fragile and brittle enough to know that complimentary words become food and drink for me. I do want people to think of me as a preacher who is effective at what he does. I want to be known as compassionate and courageous, although I know I come up short in both categories. I guess most of all I want people to think, "With his imperfections, Chuck tries to know more of who God is, and when he preaches, he wants us to know more of that God fully revealed in Jesus the Christ."

NOTHING SOUNDS THE SAME

Ecclesiastes 1:1-9
Raylean Lentz Beale

"How many is that?" she heard the nurse whisper outside her door. "Six," the doctor said in a low, troubled tone. Six miscarriages, one tubule pregnancy, and two failed adoptions.

"How many is that?" A benign question in most cases. One asked by a child, curious about the brand-new world of numbers. "How many is that?" asks the hungry college student on a midnight run to the Krispy Kreme—a simple, thoughtless, almost rote question overheard in the check out line. But to a mother whose child cannot live, nothing sounds the same. Common phrases catch her differently. Overheard comments kick up internal ironies played over in her mind. She appears absentminded to bystanders as she silently processes the magnitude of her losses. "Ma'am, could you move up?" "Next person, please." "What, oh excuse me. I'm sorry." Distracted again.

Words that were intended as comforting, explanatory, now dig. Nothing sounds the same. "God doesn't give us any more than we can handle. Where God closes a door, God opens a window." These sentiments now feel unsettling, salty, well-intended, but clichéd. With generous benefit-of-the-doubt, she tries to decide that these words have been delivered unaware by unintended carriers, whose own life experiences have allowed certain diseased meanings to lie dormant.

One "helpful" comment after another gradually reinforces her growing belief in a backhanded God. Nothing sounds the same, except maybe for the

words of our text: "Vanity of vanities, says the Teacher, vanity of vanities! All
is vanity . . . . What has been is what will be, and what has been done is what
will be done; there is nothing new under the sun." The Teacher, or
Qoheleth, in Ecclesiastes is respected, and curiously honest about what today
we call a kind of existentialist nihilism—nothing means anything and everything of perceived meaning and value eventually ends up on the "cosmic
scrap heap." Only for us (people of faith), Qoheleth eventually steps away
from a philosophical observance and into the theological arena, where he is
convinced that behind all of this vanity, utter meaninglessness, and despair,
is a God who, whether motivated by love or hate, is orchestrating it all.
Perhaps, considers our grieving mother, God is a God who backhands just
because God can.

Like Qoheleth, she gives audience to the notion that the benevolent
nature of God's divine workings cannot be confirmed. "Whether it is love or
hate one cannot know. Everything that confronts them is vanity, since the
same fate comes to all, to the righteous and the wicked, to the good and the
evil . . . as are the good so are the sinners . . ." (Eccl 9:1-2). Perhaps the musings of this wise old teacher, whom she once dismissed as cynical, depressed,
and out-of-touch, offer the only real meaning that she can accept: The
meaning is that there is no meaning. Perhaps then she can survive the death
of her child. To say that life means nothing after all spares her of the perception that all of her and her baby's efforts—to survive, bond, and be known to
each other—were for nothing.

Perhaps like the Teacher, she has come to grieve a maligned mystery. The
commentary says the kind of mystery "that cannot be made intelligible
through any of the rubrics that people usually invoke to explain the meaning" of their experiences. "Vapor," Qoheleth says thirty-eight times in the
Hebrew text, but not the kind of vapor that is short-lived and disappears.
Rather, these kinds of experiences linger with a stubborn, mocking half-life
and "make no more sense at the end" than they did in the beginning. Except
for this despondent declaration, nothing sounds the same.

In the meantime, a birthing mother's lack of control brings new life
bursting forth with joy and elation. While the miscarrying mother's lack of
control yields anguish and hopelessness, the birthing mother's pain subsides
and is given meaning by the life she has helped produce. The miscarrying
mother's pain feels punishing and unending, and means nothing save its
finger-pointing to a backhanded God. Both mothers are frightened, but the
birthing mother's fears are relieved by the cry of a child. The grieving
mother's fears are intensified by the cry of a child. Nothing means what it

meant, no one knows why these things happened, and nothing sounds the same.

Weeks, months, sometimes years pass and the declaration of the Teacher buries itself in the bunker of her heart, a heart that limps along as well as it can behind the trenches, surviving on rations of Prozac and a still unconscious hope for the cavalry. The Teacher's claim suffices—to a point. To a point it makes sense, and to a point the Prozac helps. But she begins to wonder, "Is there something beyond this point?" Like the "helpful" sentiments about God are opening windows, it makes sense to a point, but then what? Are there greater theological implications?

In the long, lonely time between, our grieving mother, at first without even noticing, inches toward the questions of her heart. They are morsels of bread leading her back to a place that used to matter. And with each step she moves away from the natural but unanswerable question of "why?" Perhaps by the Holy Spirit, perhaps by her stubborn refusal to give in to despair, perhaps by the fact that Qoheleth did not have the benefit of Jesus, somehow sacred mystery begins to take an upper hand on the maligned unknown. Like so many times before, she hunched in her bunker at the end of a long day, only this time she did not hunch alone. "May I hunch here with you?" the voice asked. In a moment of theological clarity, clarity that only this kind of suffering can bring, she knew, but she asked anyway, "Who are you?" "Blessed are the poor in spirit, for theirs is the kingdom of heaven. Blessed are those who mourn, for they will be comforted . . ." She listened to his gentle knowing, and nothing was beginning to sound the same.

He peaceably confiscated conventional wisdom, ennobling it with paradox and promise, so that the meaning which once was, he promised would not mean so for eternity. What was assumed, he promised, could be assumed no longer. For human perception is just that, and only that. And our best efforts can make it no more than perception. As she listened she began to hope that the pain of her past and the promise of her future had indeed met in the paradox of the present with a man named Jesus. He did not explain the "whys" of her pain, and some of what he said she still did not know. But she did know that her new, old friend spoke as one who had known suffering too, not hanging on a cross suffering, but suffering familiar to her. For a moment, her mind wandered about how the disciples tried to scurry the children away from him, how children drew to him, unable to keep themselves from his lap. How he and they adored one another. Yet his life would allow for none. As he hunched down beside her, she did not think to ask him about these things. In retrospect, asking would have been thickheaded and would have made no difference at all. His person and work had made the difference already, then and now. In retrospect, just being with him, having him hunker down beside her, meant more than getting answers. In retrospect, their hunkering down together was where she started to heal. With a different ear for hearing, she settled into the idea of being blessed.

Blessed *and* poor in spirit. Blessed *and* mourning. Tearful *and* hopeful. Grieving *and* joyful. Frightened *and* courageous. As she began to consider the "both/and" world of Christ where nothing was the same, she looked at Jesus and asked, "Is there anything else I need to know?" He raised his black eyebrows and a voice from heaven intervened. "I'm not backhanded," God said. Jesus smiled. She smiled back. She had heard the voice of God and was relieved rather than frightened and ashamed. And as she heard Jesus ask to be there with her, her once burning questions were relieved, unanswered but relieved.

Our young mother grieved and smiled, tears dry for now. Nothing for her will ever be the same.

The Process

Sometimes certain texts and pastoral topics seem more effectively preached from a postmodern, narrative approach. For me, this approach means telling a story about a particular fictitious person, his or her faith and dilemma, hopefully with which the listening congregation can identify. In this story, I hoped for a pastoral sermon to meet the character (and listeners) at a time of suffering, to offer something true and hopeful about the nature of God. I asked myself several questions as I wrote.

• Am I at least doing no harm? My paranoia spins off a dozen questions concerning this topic, mainly focused on misusing the pulpit. Are my motives pure? Do I hold myself to the same standards to which I hold other preachers? Have I avoided saying something that is downright stupid? (I keep a "junkectomy" page at the bottom of the sermon, where I constantly remove my "junk" from the manuscript, stuff that misuses power and corrupts the message.)

• Is it fresh, if not easy to hear, engaging enough to make the listener want to keep listening? Have I avoided clichés? For instance, I hope this sermon demonstrates the power of a "personal relationship with Jesus" without using a tired phrase that lures people into a Pavlovian daze.

- Have I avoided anything that would alienate a person giving institutional religion "one more shot"? Could such a person worship with us without being shut down by internal self-talk? Does the sermon do more than tell "what"? (A personal relationship with Jesus) Does it show "how"? (How does that relationship look in the life of a woman who cannot have children?) If I do a decent job with the "how," then hopefully the "what" will be clear, at least in retrospect.
- How can I be helpful in getting listeners in touch with the goodness of their efforts in their own faith journeys?
- Will this sermon offer a view of the nature of God that is holy? Am I saying anything unholy? (In Charles Poole's *Is Life Fair?* he uses this operational definition of unholy: thoughts unworthy of the nature of God.)
- Will listeners walk away from the sermon hearing that they matter deeply to God?
- Would God be delighted? Am I worshiping as I write?
- Will Willimon talks about his preaching professor asking, "Can anybody think of a reason why Jesus would have to die on the cross so this sermon could be preached?" Have I at least approached the magnitude and dignity of this question?

Once I knew, by the hair on the back of my neck, that the sermon needed to be told from a narrative perspective, I began writing the story. I wrote until I got stuck in a place where the character could not only no longer proceed to a deeper level of intimacy with God, but she was also in theological crisis. From there I went to the commentaries to see how the Scripture would inform her faith journey. Then I went back and rewrote the story with the benefits of Scripture and Jesus.

Working out of a place of my own doubt, for my own benefit, I had to see where her life would take her without the message of the sermon, in order to experience that despair myself, to see what difference the message of the sermon could make. It was a painful process, one that kept me up all night asking some difficult questions. One night I went downstairs to the sofa to sit alone with God and my question: "How is it that some women can have such difficulty conceiving, and my own daughter was born with less effort than it takes to order a sweater from Lands End?"

Then pastoral questions: "How can I even begin to offer a word when I am not only fertile, but also adopted by parents who tell a beautiful story about the process of getting me?" The pastoral questions took care of themselves simply by referring back to my first question regarding misuse of the pulpit and its narcissistic roots. Like the narcissism of misuse, I realized this sermon is not about me, at least not in the sense over which I am creating anxiety.

Left to the theological question of God's role in the recreation of human life, and how life occurs so easily for some and not for others, like the character in the sermon I experienced the comforting presence of God the night I sat on the sofa with my fears and questions. Determined not to sleep until I got a look back from the man whose garment I was pulling, I experienced the peace of the Holy Spirit. I got the blessing, if not the answers, and realized that the sermon at least rang true for me. In sermon writing I worry most about holy integrity, and struggle with whether anyone should ever read/hear/be subjected to my musings. That chronic worry perhaps informs the process of writing my sermons more than anything.

Raylean Lentz Beale resides in Apex, North Carolina, with her husband, Roger, and daughter, Grace. A graduate of North Carolina State University, "Ray" received her M.Div. from Duke Divinity School and is currently working on her D.Min. at Baptist Theological Seminary in Richmond, Virginia. In addition to her roles as spouse, mother, and student, Ray works as a pastoral counselor for churches in the Raleigh Baptist Association, facilitates a weekly spiritual formations group at Duke Divinity School and co-teaches the college Sunday school at Forest Hills Baptist Church in Raleigh. When Ray preached in the D.Min. class, she could have been called as our pastor if it had been a trial sermon.

SERMON IN TWO PARTS

Part 1: A God for Such a Time as This

September 16, 2001 (first Sunday after the 9-11-01 terrorist attacks)
Psalm 130—"Out of the depths I cry to you . . ."
Rhonda Van Dyke Colby

I have both longed for and dreaded this day.

I longed for it because I wanted us to be together. Just like on Tuesday I wanted to be under the same roof with members of my family, I have longed for it to be the Lord's Day, and to be together with my faith family under the same roof . . . the roof of the Lord's house.

I have wanted to see familiar and beloved faces in familiar and beloved surroundings. In a week filled with such incomprehensible events, I wanted to be together and hear the sounds of your voices singing and hear you pray prayers I have heard God's people pray over the decades.

I have longed for this day.

But, honestly, I have dreaded it as well. Week after week I am struck with the awesome privilege of bringing you a good word from God in this place. This week it is all the more awesome, but the privilege has felt like such a weighty, even impossible task. I have prayed and wondered what you would need to hear me say and what God would have me say.

Friday night I read more than 100 e-mails. Most of them were from my colleagues. We were conferencing electronically, sharing prayer concerns, names of the missing, and how our churches were responding. I read dozens of sermons my colleagues were working on for this day. Each was a unique offering. But as I read, I felt more and more inadequate. Some of my colleagues spoke with such conviction. They spoke of just war and God's vengeance and God's punishment. Some of them said there was no room in a Christian's life for fear. Others outlined the course our nation and church must take. Some pontificated about policy and politics. Some, frankly, were quick and confident as they placed blame (like that Lynchburg preacher). I envied them. I wondered where their confidence and bravado came from. Did I miss that course in seminary? Was my faith sorely lacking if I had more sorrow than answers?

So I have dreaded standing before you—knowing so little, feeling so inadequate. My prayer has been the slogan from the Children's Defense Fund: "Dear Lord, be good to me. The sea is so big and my boat is so small."

When you were in school taking an essay test, were you occasionally struck with how little you knew? You could have studied for days and might still not know the answer to the particular question the teacher was asking. You know what to do in those circumstances? When you're not sure you know the answer, tell about what you *do* know. That's what I would like to do this morning. To tell you what I *do* know.

I know that God is love. And everyone who loves has been born of God and knows God. For God is love.

I know that in God we see the holy balance between justice and mercy. Justice without mercy is barbarian. Mercy without justice ultimately is equally destructive.

I know that God sees our suffering, and that our sorrow counts to God. Psalm 56 says that God records our tears on a scroll, collects our tears in a jar. Just as it is New York's intent not to leave one person unaccounted for, God will not leave even one tear unaccounted for. Whether you have cried because you knew someone who has died or because you were afraid or because you didn't know how to answer your child's questions or because there was nothing to do but cry, every tear counts to God and every tear is accounted for.

I know that God not only sees our suffering but also *knows* our suffering firsthand. Words from Isaiah that help point us to Jesus say that he was "a man of sorrows acquainted with grief." Jesus, the flesh-form of God, grieved and cried over the death of a friend. Jesus showed not only restraint but also love to his enemies. Jesus was beaten, spit upon, humiliated, and died as if crushed by the weight of the whole world's sin. Through Jesus, God has experienced human suffering.

And I know that God has the last word. When all was chaos and the world was without form and void, God spoke and with a word brought a new creation into being. When all hope was lost and Jesus' dead body was trapped behind a boulder, God spoke a resurrection. Boulders and bombs, tombs and terrorists are never the last word. They won't have the last word this time either. God has a way that I do not understand. I don't understand it, but I recognize it when I see it. God has a way of reaching into the ruin and rubble and wrenching grief and bringing forth a resurrection.

In the days that have followed Tuesday's atrocities, healthy babies have been born, six-year-olds have lost their first teeth, our friend got miraculously good news from the oncologist. A young couple got married here yesterday. People who were estranged from one another have picked up the phone to say, "I love you." None of these things will undo what some extremists did on Tuesday. But extremists cannot silence God. And God is not finished yet. That much I know.

God is love . . . a faithful balance of justice and mercy, acquainted with suffering, and God will always have the last word. I'm sure of these things. That doesn't sound like much in a time such as this. But in a strange kind of way, in this week when so much has been unsure, it has been enough.

Part 2: A People for Such a Time as This
Romans 12:9-21—*"Do not be overcome by evil, but overcome evil by doing good."*

We have a God for such a time as this. Almost as surely as I know that, I know that we are a people for such a time as this.

The Church of Jesus Christ is made up of individuals who are completely human. That means we get angry. That means we get afraid. There is nothing shameful or un-Christian about what you are feeling. What you are feeling is neither good nor bad. But while our feelings may be ethically neutral, how we act on them is ethically crucial.

Listen to these words: "Happy is the one who repays you for what you have done to us—he who seizes your infants and dashes them against the rocks!" Shocking language! Are they the words of political extremists or true patriots? They are the words of the 137th Psalm. God knows that we feel rage and that our human nature desires vengeance. But the word of God says, "Do not pay back evil for evil but overcome evil by doing good."

If we stoop to vengeance and violence, if we turn with suspicion against our neighbor, if we start to suspect people because of their names or religion, then terrorism has won. Then terrorism has collapsed more than centers of trade and power. Then terrorism has collapsed the image of Christ that is growing up inside of us. When our insides begin to look more like them than like Christ, terrorism has won.

So how are we a people for such a time as this? We are a people for such a time as this because we know that love is stronger than death. We are a people for such a time as this because fifty-two weeks out of every year we are singing and praying and working to turn the tide of hatred and intolerance toward a place we do not yet fully see, a place called the Kingdom of God, a place where lions and lambs lie down together, where spears are not necessary and are reforged into pruning hooks. We are a people for such a time as this because we have worked to make this place (God's house) open to everyone—to the community, to the homeless, to the Christian and non-Christian, to the addict and the alien.

We are a people for such a time as this because years before we were in a new kind of war, we began waging a new kind of peace. Laura Stough, a third grader who has been raised most of her life in our church heard about and saw some of the horror of Tuesday. It was very upsetting to her. Laura passionately asked, "Why hasn't someone taught these people peace? Why isn't someone going right now to teach them?" Why indeed, Laura. We are a people for just such a time as this.

We are waging a new kind of peace—

where differences are not so much threatening as enlightening;

where children learn to approach conflict with heart and mind and not fists and weapons.

where listening and compassion are not passive virtues but are active skills worth learning, developing, and practicing.

where justice is sought before there is any need of vengeance.

where sorrow may tarry for a night but joy comes in the morning.

where love is sincere.

where the only thing we hate is evil.

where we are devoted to one another in brotherly and sisterly love.

where we honor one another above ourselves.

where we never lack in zeal and we always keep our fervor serving the Lord.

where we are joyful and hopeful, patient in affliction, and faithful in prayer.

where we share with God's people who are in need.

where we practice hospitality.

where we bless those who persecute us, bless and do not curse them.

where we rejoice with those who rejoice and mourn with those who mourn.

where we live in harmony with one another and associate with people of low degree.

where we do not repay anyone evil for evil, but do what is right.

where as far as it depends on us, we live at peace with everyone.

Friends—Bon Air United Methodist Church—we are waging a new kind of peace. We are a people for such a time as this.

We are sowers of seeds of peace. We are sanctuaries of solace. We are workers for justice. We are harbingers of hope. We are the instruments of God's peace, for such a time as this.

Reflections on the Preaching Task

Pastoral ministry has taught me the importance of authentic preaching. I have learned that, given the choice, listeners would rather a preacher be authentic than authoritative. While clear biblical teaching is important to listeners, they long to hear not only the preacher's conclusions, but his or her journey as well.

Early in my ministry, with courses in biblical exegesis fresh in my mind, I wanted to deliver an objective, eternal truth to listeners. However, while preaching unshakable surety, instead of feeling confident I felt fraudulent. I sometimes spoke in convincing ways about things of which I was not convinced. Over time I learned that being open about my own struggle with a text or occasion made my preaching more natural and more honest. Doing so did not undermine my authority. It seemed to invite others to their own authentic encounter with God's Word.

On a weekly basis I have to resist the temptation to move too quickly toward the commentaries and lectionary study books. Those tools are part of my preparation, but when I consult them too soon I avoid dealing personally with the text. To truly understand a text I must stand under that text. I must allow the biblical word to pour over me. I must be still enough to let it soak into me, to seek out the dry places in my soul and make its way to where my hurts and hopes are hiding. The first step in sermon preparation, then, is a devotional one. It is to read the word in the very presence of God and to listen to the whispers between my pains and passions and divine purpose.

Often this initial encounter leads me to understand the "ouch" in the human condition that cries out for the word of that particular text. While the text is the starting point for study, the aching question in the human condition is often the starting place for creating a sermon.

During the week of September 11, 2001, I did not first run to the triumphant and victorious words of Scripture. Instead I was drawn to biblical laments. I looked there for reassurances that God understood terror, devastation, and despair. I looked there for ancient words to wrap around our current condition, because my own words failed me at every turn.

The week unfolded with special services of prayer and remembrance. Pastors everywhere were on "high alert." The Sunday sermon loomed large on the horizon of a chaotic week. I looked to friends and trusted colleagues to be sources of wisdom and clarity. As I read e-mails and internet reflections I was struck with how quickly some preachers had clarity about what we were experiencing. I was taken aback and even intimidated by their authoritative interpretation of world events. Hungrily I read the words of others. I am sure that their thoughts and phrases found their way into my sermon. I longed to possess what enabled them to speak with such authority. Instead I decided that the only way for me to speak an authentic word was to share my struggle as a part of the sermon.

What resulted was an understated message. I took a minimalist approach. Focusing on the simple and sure seemed to help those who were feeling frantic and anxious. I know it helped me to stay close to the calm center where God resides.

Comfort, however, was not all that needed to be spoken. Yes, people were traumatized and needed a reassuring word from their faith. However, I thought to speak only comfort would be to reinforce a victim identification. I felt called to speak a word of challenge as well as comfort. I wanted to speak to people's strengths and not just to their trauma.

Assuming that people under stress have shortened attention spans, I decided to preach the sermon in two parts and to underscore each section with music that reinforced the message. The first part was the minimalist approach focusing on what we know about God. It was followed by an anthem that cried for God's gracious mercy. In the second part I tried to challenge the collective body by speaking to the strength of the church over time. It seemed particularly appropriate to have the congregation hear the echoes of its own strength and witness through the words of a child raised in their midst. There was a crescendo in the cadence of the second section. At its height a very simple rendition of the Prayer of St. Francis was sung. The prayer seemed confident and simple. When a third grade girl sang the final verse, there was a tangible sense of hope for the future.

During the days that preceded that Sunday, I thought back to what I was taught in seminary. I remembered my evangelism professor saying every sermon should provide an opportunity for someone to come to faith for the first time. I remembered my ethics professor saying every sermon text is a social justice text. I remembered my preaching professor telling me to weave the biblical story, the preacher's story, and the listeners' stories together.

I tried to think like a seminary-trained preacher. But I knew that on this Sunday, like every other Sunday, it was most important for me to approach the sermon task first as a sinner in need of grace, a pilgrim in need of direction, a beggar in search of bread. Only then can homiletical tools be instruments of an authentic word. The preacher is a vessel through which the word comes, but the vessel itself must be shaped and reshaped by what it carries . . . the living, pulsating word of God. That word has the power to transform the preacher and the listener.

Authentic preaching invites the preacher, the individual listener, and the congregation to sojourn together as their faith is deepened and their lives changed by God's grace. Years ago an elderly church member commented regularly on my sermons. He occasionally left the service saying, "I think that was a good sermon. I'll let you know in a year or so. I'll know for sure if it makes a difference in the way I live."

Rhonda Van Dyke Colby is senior minister at the Bon Air United Methodist Church in Richmond, Virginia. A gifted preacher and pastor, Rhonda is actively involved in the community. Her husband, Donald, is also a United Methodist minister in the Richmond area. Rhonda and Don have two sons and a daughter. Rhonda graduated from James Madison University in Virginia and Wesley Seminary in Washington, DC. Among her teachers was Dr. Edmund Steimle, well-known in the area of homiletics. Rhonda is now working on her doctor of ministry degree at Baptist Theological Seminary in Richmond. Those of us who teach at BTSR are delighted to have this winsome Wesleyan influence.

OUR FIRST LOVE

Genesis 1:26-31; 1 John 4:7-11
Stephen Hunter Cook

BRIDE and GROOM, you have invited us here today as family and friends not simply to witness your marriage, but to participate with you in this service of worship. We rejoice today because you have chosen to come to this place, this sanctuary in which we offer ourselves to God in worship, and to be united in holy matrimony. Anytime that the community of faith gathers to worship, we recognize that what we are doing is not simply putting on some sort of show that we hope will be pleasing to God. Nor is it dressing up and merely acting a part. It is not something that we do because we are perfect or because we are faultless in our faith, for we are far from it. Rather, when we come to the sanctuary to worship, we come to offer ourselves—our faults and our frailties, our worries and our weaknesses. We come to this place to remind ourselves again of the God who has created us and who loves us; the God in whose image we have been made and who, in the person of Jesus Christ, has shown us the image of love that knows no end. That is why we come to worship. Because we are loved by a God who loves so extravagantly that God would become susceptible to every circumstance we face, and to embody love in its purest form.

BRIDE and GROOM, some of what we see in you and your love for one another is the kind of love that God has revealed to us. We celebrate with you because you have found one another. BRIDE, you have found GROOM, and you are here today to pledge your steadfast love and faithfulness to him in marriage. And GROOM, you have found BRIDE, and you are here today to pledge your steadfast love to her in marriage. That is a covenant that you are making with one another, a commitment you are making in the company of those who are closest to you that will endure for the rest of your lives. It is the kind of commitment that assures your beloved of your love and faithfulness. It is the kind of commitment that God has made with each of us since the beginning of time. In the very first verses of the Bible, we hear the details of how God goes about the work of creating the world. Each day God speaks and something new is made. And each day God looks at what has just been formed and says that it is good. On the sixth day, Genesis tells us, God creates humankind in God's own image. And while everything else that has been created has been called good, God sees in humans something more, and God blesses humankind and says that it is very good.

BRIDE and GROOM, it is very good that you have come to this place today to unite with one another and to create a new life together. In the same way that God's self has been wedded to this world since the beginning of time—a union born out of a love that knows no end—you are here today to wed yourselves to one another. And while God may have said that the creation of humans was indeed very good, God never mistook us for being perfect. God knows that we come up short in many parts of our lives much of the time. You both will work together in your marriage, and you both will give all that you have to the other. Yet you both will come up short in many places much of the time, and you both will let the other down. But in the same way that God never gives up on any one of us, so you too should never give up on the other. What you are embarking on is a journey of discovery. You will discover things about your spouse that you could have never imagined in your relationship up to now. You will discover things about yourself that you would have no knowledge of if it weren't for this one who is pledging to be your life's partner. In some things you will find that your backgrounds are more diverse than you had first suspected, while in other situations you will see that there could never be another with whom you could hold so much in common.

But even while opinions may differ and dreams may have to be renegotiated more often than you would like, you will discover that there is but one thing that is the cornerstone of your marriage: the love that you share for God as you see it revealed in one another. Much of what we find in the pages of Scripture are attempts that the ancestors of our faith made to describe God and the nature of God's love. In the New Testament, John's first letter says that we cannot separate God and love; the two are one in the same. And because of that, the writer says, "everyone who loves is born of God and knows God" (4:7b). BRIDE and GROOM, as you have discovered your love for one another, you have seen more of what it means to be loved by God. You remind all of us who are gathered here today of our own covenants of love that we have created with God and with one another. We pledge our love and our prayers for you; it is our most sincere hope that your love for one another will continue to grow from this day forward. And even more, it is our prayer that you will continue to find the One who has created you, whose grace has united you, and whose love has been yours since the beginning of time and continues for you now and forever. Amen.

Pastoral Preaching in the Context of a Wedding

Both in the church and in the larger cultural context in which we live, it is widely recognized that marriage is one of the most significant life transitions that people ever experience. In recent history, we have seen weddings evolve into grandiose productions that take months and even years of planning to "pull off." As ministers, we never know quite what to expect when a couple calls and asks us if we will preside at their wedding. Ask any pastor who has ever officiated at a wedding, and you will hear some of the bizarre things that people want us to do in their efforts to make their special day unforgettable for everyone involved. Like funerals, weddings often provide ministers the opportunity to interact with people who ordinarily would have nothing to do with the church. Even those people who have never had any meaningful relationship with a congregation will often call on the local church's pastor to officiate at their wedding. The union of two lives in marriage is something so momentous that some of the people most disinterested in matters of faith and religion recognize the significance of the journey they are embarking on and the role that the church can play in helping them begin their new lives together. As ministers, we must regularly ask ourselves, What message do we have to proclaim when we stand before a couple and a congregation and preside over the public union of two lives?

While funerals are generally understood to be the services in the life of the church that address people's issues of grief, weddings do not come without their own moments of angst. A wedding is a unique blend of excitement and anxiety, hope and fear, celebration and grief. Issues arise around the time of a marriage that put people's emotions close to the surface. Tears are not an uncommon sight when the doors at the back of the church swing open and the bride makes her way down the aisle, because we are all too aware that this marks not only the beginning of a new way of life for a couple and their families, but it also signals an end to old ways of relating for everyone involved. Whenever "a man leaves his father and his mother and clings to his wife, and they become one flesh" (Gen 2:24), they are crafting a new way of relating with their world, a way that replaces "I" with "we." Because of that, the ways in which people interact are changing for everyone who witnesses the marriage. As ministers, we know that wherever there is change, no matter how wonderful and welcome this may be, there is also grief. Grief is as much a part of the marriage of two people as it is any other life-changing event. While the union of a bride and groom may provide cause for great celebration, there is still the fact that one way of life is ending and a new and uncertain way of life is beginning. We who are pastors stand at the intersection of what was and what will be, and we are called to speak a word on behalf of God in the midst of it all.

Ministers at weddings play a unique role unlike any other they are called on to play in the congregation. In officiating at a marriage, ministers function on behalf of the state and yet operate out of the authority that has been invested in them by God and formalized in their ordination. Therefore, it is important that ministers recognize this is not merely some ceremony in which they "perform" some part. Rather, this is a service of worship in which we as ministers are pointing people's attention beyond the people surrounding them and to the presence of God in our midst.

Insuring that the wedding is truly a service of worship and not simply a production put on by overzealous families is one of the most difficult tasks ministers face in officiating at a marriage. Recognizing that we are speaking to a congregation comprised of a bride and groom, as well as family and friends who have varying degrees of affiliation with the church, we begin to see the many different factors that we must take into account as we shape our words for this occasion. It is important that we begin our work with the engaged couple well in advance of the event in order to speak personal words crafted from the experiences we have had of relating with this man and woman in previous encounters.

Usually I require any couple that asks me to preside at their wedding to take part in at least three counseling sessions, although four or five is preferable. In our first meeting, I emphasize the importance not simply of planning a service, but of building a marriage centered in Christian faith. Once we lay that foundation, we devote time to discussing the order of worship for their wedding day. During that time, I provide them with a copy of the entire service that includes every word I will say. Unlike other settings in which I may speak as a minister, I think it is important to have every part of the service written out for the couple in advance for at least three reasons. First, in the midst of pulling together the different details involved with planning a wedding, it helps calm their fears about what will be going on during that part of the day. This insures that they do not have to worry about being surprised by anything I will say. Second, I know that the couple will have a hard enough time standing up through the whole event, even without having to comprehend what I am saying. By giving them this piece in advance, there may be some familiar word or phrase that catches their attention during the service that will help ease some of their anxiety. Finally, and most importantly, I provide the couple with a copy of the words I will speak because it affords me the opportunity to remind them again of the purpose for our gathering and the significance of their decision to marry.

As pastors, we must always be alert to teachable moments, and weddings are full of those types of educational opportunities. While it may be true that the bride and groom will have a hard time hearing what we say to them during the service itself, I still make sure in the homily that my words are directed to them. Families and friends who comprise the congregation for that day play a vital role in the couple's being there, and that certainly needs to be acknowledged. If there are times when certain family members can be included in other parts of the service, then that is worth exploring. At the very least, it is important that the minister says something at the outset of the service to recognize the love and care of those gathered to witness the event. Then in the homily, I speak with the awareness that there are others present not only to overhear what I say to the couple, but also to worship God. It is a time in which we all are reminded of the responsibilities we hold in common by living our lives in relationship with God and one another. The homily and the whole service afford us all the opportunity to renew old covenants even as we form new ones. Commitment is the theme for the day. I am convinced that the church has something vitally important to say on such issues as sharing life with another person, starting a home, beginning a family, and redefining the relationships that nurture and shape us. When we as ministers stand before a congregation and speak about such things as love, commitment, faithfulness, and trust, and when we pronounce two people husband and wife, it is a defining moment for everyone gathered to worship

Stephen Hunter Cook is in his third and final year as a student at Baptist Theological Seminary in Richmond, Virginia. An honors graduate of Wake Forest University, Stephen currently serves as moderator of the student government association at the seminary. After his first year at the seminary, Stephen was selected for the John Grover Scales Preaching Award, an award that recognizes the gifts and potential of a student in preaching. Stephen currently serves as pastoral intern at Derbyshire Baptist Church in Richmond. In 2002, Stephen was married to Amy Christen Costantini, who is a student at BTSR and associate moderator of the student government association. Their union represents the biggest merger of power in the short history of BTSR.

A FUNERAL SERMON FOR HERMAN WEBB

Phillip Reynolds

It is our tradition to mark someone's dying with a funeral or memorial service, or both. We do this because it is important for family and friends to release the one who has died and let that person make his final, ultimate rite of passage, the passage into eternity. There are two tasks before us today: to remember well and honestly the life and legacy of Herman Webb and to attend to the grief and sorrow of this family and these friends.

Herman Webb—a father, a father-in-law, a grandfather, and a friend. Also a wonderful, steadfast, faithful husband (more about his married life in a few moments). But what else? A good Christian man, servant of Christ, and teacher of the Bible. Herman Webb was also an astute businessman and a successful one. He was a success both behind the scenes as a department store buyer and behind the counter, dealing directly with customers, as he opened and operated the Diamond Brand Camping supply store in Fletcher, North Carolina, near Hendersonville. That store gave Herman Webb a place to really show what he could do. Every man wants to be successful at some kind of work in the world, and Herman was an unqualified success managing Diamond Brand. He opened it, operated it, and expanded it. It is still there today, decades after his retirement, still thriving and growing. It is as if some of the words of Psalm 1 are put to life in Herman Webb:

Blessed is the man who does not walk in the counsel of the wicked, or stand in the way of sinners or sit in the seat of the mockers. But his delight is in the law of the LORD, and on his law he meditates day and night. He is like a tree planted by streams of water, which yields its fruit in season and whose leaf does not wither. Whatever he does prospers.

"Whatever he does prospers." That is true in the life of Herman Webb, a righteous businessman who operated his store in a good, decent, Christian manner.

However, material success and business success are *not* the measure of a man's life. They are not the things that are of eternal importance. How we relate to God, our family, and friends *are* the most important things. In these areas Herman Webb was truly remarkable. He gave his only child, his daughter Buelah, a good, loving, nurturing home in which to grow up, and he continued his love for his daughter all of his life. For Wendell, his son-in-law, he provided acceptance, encouragement, wisdom, kindness, and love. For his grandchildren, Catherine and Kevin, he was a source of joy, love, and friendship. In addition, his friendship extended beyond his family to his work, his church, and his community.

Nevertheless, his relationship with his wife, Bessie Mae Webb, was extraordinary. When Herman Webb said his wedding vows, evidently he meant them. For him, "for better, for worse, for richer or poorer, in sickness and in health, till death us do part" meant exactly what it said. Herman thought married folks were supposed to take care of one another their whole married lives, no matter what. Many of you know the story—how Mrs. Webb became ill with Alzheimer's disease and Herman cared for her in their home for over seven years.

Seven years! There is something symbolic in that. Seven is the biblical number for completeness. It is a shorthand literary symbol that means all the way, totally, and completely. When Herman cared for his wife for seven years, it says of him that he cared for Bessie Mae all the way, totally, and completely.

I know that memorial services tend to be saccharine and falsely make heroes of the deceased, but let's be honest, there was something quietly heroic in what Herman did for Bessie Mae. Many of you know so much more about this than I. People like the Webbs' friends and doctor, Dr. James Ebersole, can tell you what it is like to care for, around the clock, an Alzheimer patient. Often these quiet, heroic efforts that people like Herman perform for their loved ones go unnoticed by the world, but not this case. There was a newspaper feature article on what Herman did, and a television news story about his care for his wife. Herman's caregiving became so well known that it was used as a case study in medical school and it helped shape the Family Practice Program for physicians in residency at Richland Memorial Hospital.

Herman Webb, quite a gentleman, wouldn't we say? Husband, father, grandfather, businessman, churchman, and friend. His dying is a sad loss for so many. For his family, it is our prayer that you are finding and will find God's comfort in your sadness and grief. Live in the comfort of these and so many other good memories of this man. Find comfort in the fact that you are proud of Herman—who he was and how he lived. Moreover, allow yourselves the comfort of knowing that as a daughter, Buelah, and also Wendell, Kevin, and Catherine, you did well in your care of Herman, just as he did for Bessie Mae. Your care would have spanned seven years, too, if need be. You know it's true.

Above all, let God's Spirit and God's promise comfort you. God's healing is not just for illness and broken limbs but for broken hearts as well. Jesus' promises are today for you: "Blessed are you who mourn," he said, "for you shall be comforted." You will be, you will be. First comes the mourning, and Christ mourns with you today. My favorite picture of Jesus was when he stood and wept with Mary and Martha at the death of their brother Lazarus. So, too, he weeps with you today.

And just as he blessed Lazarus with new life, he will surely raise Herman to eternal life. "I am the resurrection and life; he who believes in me, though he may die yet shall he live."

Herman Webb shall live.

Preparing for the Funeral Sermon

During my first year as a pastor a woman said to me, "If I go to all the trouble to die, I hope some preacher will see fit to say a few nice things about me instead of using my funeral to try to save everybody." She was funny, blunt, and she had a point. I have never forgotten it. What is the function of the funeral sermon? It is to help the family accept the fact that their loved one has died; it is a time to remember and celebrate his or her life, and it is a time for the pastor to restate the promises of Jesus Christ that can bring comfort to the family in their grief. That is a pretty tall order, and it is enough to fill the funeral service. We need not feel obligated to further fill the already full agenda by pointedly preaching evangelism. The good news will be included when claiming the promise of Christ's resurrection for all who believe in him. Therefore, we are free to "see fit to say a few nice things" about the one who has died.

But how does one know what to say? The family will provide the content of the eulogy. All the preacher needs to do is to go to the family, express love and sympathy, and then take a seat and *listen.* In my experience, very little prompting is needed. Family and close friends have always seemed eager to talk about the one who has died. Stories and memories come pouring forth. Usually there is much laughter and quite a lot of dabbing tears from corners of eyes as the remembrances are recounted, one after another.

I cannot say enough about this visit. It is of extreme importance for the pastor as he or she gets a feel for what to say at the upcoming funeral, but it is more than that. In a very real sense, this visit *is* the funeral for the family. Never hurry through this visit. Usually I try to find a seat where most everyone can see me. They need someone to whom they can direct their comments. They are not talking to inform one other, but are performing an important function of celebration. It is as if they are saying of a particular aspect of the deceased's life, "This needs to be said of my mother. Let's dare not forget this about her." Everyone else in the room already knows what "this" is, so nothing new is being told. But something important is being verbalized in this act of retelling. The preacher is wise to do more listening than anything else during this visit. He or she is not there to make pain go away, or to theologize about life, death, sin, and salvation. The stories the family celebrates together have more healing power than the preacher's words at this point. The important function the preacher performs is creating a reason and an opportunity to let the family celebrate the life that has gone from them.

When the preacher leaves this visit, he or she should know what is most important to say in the funeral sermon about the one who has died. There will be certain stories that beg to be retold, or certain peculiarities that are too precious to ignore. These aspects of the person's life will constitute the eulogy portion of the pastor's remarks and will make up the bulk of the funeral sermon.

The preacher is now ready to deal with the family's need for comfort in the funeral sermon. Comfort will come to the family in three ways. First, the family will find great comfort in their shared memories and stories of the one who has died. This has already happened during the pastor's visit and preaching the eulogy portion of the sermon, but the pastor should encourage the family to continue to tell and retell these stories. Second, comfort comes in the truth of the resurrection. The preacher may want to focus on passages in 1 Corinthians 15, 1 Thessalonians 4, Revelation 21, and the words of Jesus in the John 11, or other references in the Bible. Third, the preacher can remind the family of Jesus Christ's promises of comfort directly to them as Christ's Spirit works to comfort their grieving hearts. This is promised in the Beatitudes, described as the work of the Holy Spirit in John 14–16, and spoken of by Paul in the opening chapter of 2 Corinthians. By eulogizing the life of the one who "went to all the trouble to die," sharing the healing power of shared memories, sharing the truth of the resurrection, and emphasizing the work of the Spirit to comfort us in our grief, the preacher will have provided the family with the opportunity to say good-bye properly and to begin the journey of adjusting to their loss. And that would enough to do in one single sermon.

Phillip Reynolds has been pastor of the Kathwood Baptist Church in Columbia, South Carolina, for eleven years. Phillip was among the first students to complete the D.Min. degree at Baptist Theological Seminary. Phillip and his wife Betsy have four children. Phillip is active in moderate Baptist life and in the life of his community. Among Phillip's hobbies are jogging. Phillip likes to run fast but has been known to slow down to allow wheezing seminary professors to keep pace.

THE CALL TO DARING DISCIPLESHIP

Luke 9:57-62
Charles Bugg

Luke has a way of slipping the most extraordinary words into what seem like ordinary times. "As they were walking along"—Jesus and his followers were walking along, and some people expressed interest in joining his movement. New members for the church! I get excited about people joining the church. It helps my reputation as a preacher. I don't say things like, "Foxes have holes and birds of the air have their nests, but the Son of Man has nowhere to lay his head." I say, "Welcome to the church. What can we do for you? How can we make you feel at home?"

Jesus doesn't say that. His response is a jarring reminder that the call to follow him is the ultimate decision of life. Jesus takes this seriously. "Follow me," Jesus says. "Lord, just let me go and bury my father." That sounds like a reasonable request. We all preach family values. But Jesus replied, "Let the dead bury their own dead, but you go and proclaim the kingdom of God."

What's going on with Jesus? Where's the love? Where's the sympathy? I know some biblical commentators say that the man's father really wasn't dead. The father is sick, and his son is trying to weasel out of following Jesus. "I'll stay with my dad until he dies, and then I'll try to find you, Jesus, if you're still around."

But let's not tame the text to make Jesus appear kinder and gentler. Something big is happening. Jesus says proclaiming the kingdom is more important than burying our parents.

We understand this better when we know where Jesus is in his own life. A few verses before Luke says Jesus set his face toward Jerusalem. Jesus is on the move, and he knows what awaits him. He's on the road, and the road leads to his own death. Sometimes in our lives small talk won't do. "How's the family? I'll be glad when it gets warmer. Have a merry little Christmas." My own conversation is filled with that kind of chatter. I suppose it's necessary. We don't want to greet everybody with, "If you died tonight, do you know where you'll spend eternity?" That's too heavy. People start to avoid us.

"What do you think of the weather?" That's a question that demands little thought unless you're a meteorologist.

But when you know you're going to die soon; when you know the death will be painful; when you have the sense that what you're living and dying for are at the heart of life, then you speak in ways that reflect that importance. All pastors know the scene. I would drive to the hospital to see someone who had been diagnosed with cancer. What would I say? What reassurance could I give? "I know the doctors say it's terminal, but I pray that God will heal you." I so much wanted to say that, but I knew that like so many things we face, this wasn't in my hands. When I walked into the room, I didn't start the conversation. She did. "Pastor, I'm afraid. I don't want to die. But if I do, I've been thinking about what really is important. Whatever days I have, I want to love God more, tell my husband and girls I love them so much. I want to do what makes a difference."

Would you understand if I said that in some ways I envied her? I didn't envy the disease. I didn't envy the chemotherapy. I didn't envy her probably never seeing her daughters graduate from high school or seeing them get married. But I did envy her grasp of what seemed crucial and central to life. For her, time had changed. No longer could important words be delayed. She had this moment, and maybe a few more ticks of the clock. "Pastor, I'm afraid . . . I want to do what makes a difference."

I suppose death does that for us. Life becomes tightened and more focused. There's little time for small talk. I want to speak about love, forgiveness, peace, eternity—in short, I want to speak about the things that ultimately make all the difference.

Jesus is on the way to Jerusalem. Some people call this text part of the "travel narrative" of Luke. Yet, this is hardly what I call travel. It's a death march. It's Jesus' journey to Jerusalem. Jesus is going to Gethsemane and Golgotha, and even in the early part of the travel, we smell death.

Three men want to follow Jesus. What a compliment. Three more disciples as this traveling salvation show moves toward Jerusalem. "I will follow you, Lord; but first let me go back and say good-bye to my family." That sounds reasonable. More family values. The Jews cherish family, and all these last two want to do is go home, one to bury his father and the other to say good-bye. I don't know a sensible church or a sensitive minister that wouldn't say, "Take care of your house." These would-be disciples seem sincere. There's not a thing in this episode that indicates they didn't want to follow Jesus. "I'll say good-bye to my family and then I'll follow." Jesus replied, "No one who puts his hand to the plow and looks back is fit for service in the kingdom of God."

They didn't understand how ultimate and how urgent the call to follow Jesus was. I understand these men. I live as if there's always more time to do the things that are really important. If I have a student who doesn't get an assignment in on time, I want to be understanding. "My father has died. I need to be home with my family." "Of course," I reply, "that's where you should be. Learning to proclaim the kingdom of God can wait."

Maybe, though, I shouldn't be so understanding. After all, Jesus says, "Let the dead bury their own dead, but you go and proclaim the kingdom of God." Really, that seems to me to be a good way to guarantee a small following. It sounds fanatical. It doesn't make sense. It's offensive.

Recently, the Richmond newspaper ran several articles on trends in religion today. Do you know what the writers said? The good news is there's an increased interest in spirituality. People want to know more about God. However, the bad news is that this spirituality often expresses itself in individuality and in a consumer's approach to church.

In other words, people want to know God. But they're not very interested in church or community and when they look for a place to express their faith, do you know what many people are asking? "What's in it for me? Tell me what Jesus can do for me. Tell me how your church can meet my needs, and then maybe I'll join."

Sounds self-centered to me. I know how radical Jesus' words seem about following him, but perhaps it's time for a course corrective in our faith. Somebody is staring death in the face and is talking about what ultimately matters. It's urgent. The journey is now. The sacrifice is now. Preaching is now. No excuses. No reasons for not doing it. "I want to bury my father." "I want to tell the family good-bye." Sorry! It's now or never.

I don't want to sound preachy. I'm talking to us, the Church. I'm sharing with you and me. Let's look at the world. Across the world, people are being killed, many of them in the name of religion. Will we speak now or wait? Mothers and fathers watch their children die from hunger. Will we speak now or wait? In the United States, the rich get richer, and many of our citizens can't afford the basics of life like medical insurance. Will we speak now or wait? People all around us need the faith that we have. Will we proclaim the kingdom now or will we wait?

In Luke's Gospel, Jesus seems to be walking, and it's all very ordinary. Three men ask if they can join. Then, the extraordinary breaks through. "Do you know where I'm going? Jerusalem! Do you have any idea what that means? Death! This journey is too important. Get in line—now or never."

THE GOD WHO WANTS IT ALL

Genesis 22:1-5
Charles Bugg

Some passages of Scripture are fairly easy to preach. The message is straightforward. The people in the story do the right things. The way God works is clear, and it all makes for a pleasant story with a nice ending.

Unfortunately, this passage in Genesis doesn't fit that mold. It does have a nice ending. Abraham and his son Isaac come down from the mountain. But on the way to this happy conclusion, the story raises a lot of questions.

Perhaps the most fundamental question it raises is about the place of God in human suffering. No other issue is faced more by a pastor. Why? Why did this happen? Why did this happen to my family and me? Why do these kinds of tragedies happen to anybody? Where is God?

In Genesis 22, it's easy to find God. "Some time later God tested Abraham," the story begins. God initiates what happens. Abraham is to take his only son Isaac to the region of Moriah, take Isaac up the mountain, and then Abraham takes the knife and is prepared to slit his son's throat for God's sake.

What do we do with a story like this? We can try to tame it. What's happening is foreshadowing, that's all. Later, the parent God would let the son Jesus die on a cross, but Abraham and Isaac—it's just a little taste of what's to come.

Another way to take the story is to say, "This is the right response to a bad religious practice in Abraham's culture." Other religions sacrificed children to their idols, but not the faith of Abraham. While Abraham gets right to the moment of offering his son, notice he doesn't. The Hebrew Scriptures are saying that taking the life of a child isn't what Yahweh wants.

Some people want to make this a simple story of obedience to God. The preacher says, "Do you love God more than you would love to have a Lexus?" We say, "Yes." Do you love God more than you would love to own the Hope diamond? Yes? Do you love God more than a husband or wife? The questions get harder. Well, yes I love God and I love my wife, but aren't we talking about loves that are compatible? Do you love God more than you love your child? What I want you to do, Abraham, is to take your only son, Isaac, the son whom you love, up the mountain of sacrifice. "This is the test," God says.

The problem with making this a simple story of obedience is that all kinds of feelings are set off in those who read the story. For example, I have two children. What if God asked me to murder one of them to prove my love for the divine?

If this story in Genesis needs more complication, remember Isaac was born when his mother Sarah was 90, and his father was 100. Isaac means laughter because Sarah said the prospect of giving birth makes me laugh and can you imagine how my friends are going to howl when I tell them the news. If Sarah's friends gave her a shower, it was probably held in the recreation room of the nursing home. But when Isaac was born, no child could have been more wanted and loved.

Male children were the future for Israel. Isaac was Abraham and Sarah's future. God said, "The test is to kill your future." Hardly a simple story of obedience. Let's face it. Those of us who are preachers can't neatly wrap this episode and package it in some sermon. This story has jagged edges, complexities, and evokes all kinds of feelings in us.

What I want to say is that this is a complicated story of obedience to God. For me, obeying God has never been simple. For instance, you and I are told to obey God's will. Well, how do I discern that will? Following God is risky. Maybe some folks have it down to a science, but I've made decisions in God's name wondering if I was doing the right thing. I've done some things and made some decisions in my life based not on sight but on intuitive faith.

Obedience is sticky and complex. In fact, it's not even a popular word these days. Remember when couples took their marriage vows. Looking at each other: "We promise to love, honor, and *obey*." Not anymore. I don't blame these couples. I haven't used the word "obey" in a marriage ceremony for a long time. Respect, trust, encourage—these are all good words, but obey reminds us when we didn't do our homework and the teacher dressed us down for not obeying orders.

I had a second-career student who had been in the Army. Whenever he talked to me, he would call me "Sir." "Sir, may I ask a question?" "Dr. Bugg, sir, I didn't understand this part of the book." One day privately and I pray gently, I said I appreciate the respect. I told him we'd taught our children when they were younger to say, "Yes sir," and "No ma'am." But I said, "I think you're overdoing the 'sir' bit. I'm not the commander, this isn't the Army, and at ease, soldier."

"Obedience" is complicated even when we use the word in church. How many folks will flock to the sanctuary to hear a sermon about "The Obedient Life"? Try "The Happy Life," "The Fulfilled Life," or "The Successful Life." But "The Obedient Life"? Besides, what are we going to say to the congregation? Do you love God? Do you love God more than you love your children or your grandchildren? Well, let me tell you about this father named Abraham . . . We don't do that. Most of us ministers are content if the people come, if they give enough money to meet the budget, and we have enough workers for the nursery.

I don't pretend to have answers to why God tested Abraham this way. It's certainly different from the image of God I preach. Words like grace, acceptance, forgiveness, unconditional love—this is my vocabulary. I look at people as if we are all struggling in some way. We need help on the journey. The faith I preach talks often about the God who is for us and with us.

Maybe that is the problem. Not that we don't need the word that God loves us. Not that we don't need to internalize the love of God for us. And certainly not that we don't want people to understand that the God of the Bible is with us and for us.

But if that's our whole message, haven't we left out something big? Does God ever challenge us? Or put another way, does God ever ask of us something that seems so outlandish, so incredible, so beyond our capabilities? Does God ever disturb our peace?

Let's face it. The Abraham and Isaac story demands a response. We either have to toss it out of our biblical canon, defuse and domesticate it, or we have to take it so seriously that the story disturbs us so much that we see a new vision of God.

God—that's really the story. Isaac and Abraham and what they do aren't the big story here. It's God. It's a God so big who comes to ask so much that, humanly speaking, it seems so incredible. What kind of God is this? It's certainly not a God we fully comprehend. It's not a God we contain or explain. It's a God who is *the* God! "What's the best you have to give, Abraham? Isaac! Isaac, your son, your only son whom you love, your future, the child of promise, the boy who makes Sarah and you laugh and who brings tears of pride to your eyes. Bring Isaac to me."

Each year we have a stewardship campaign in the church. I know most of us hate to talk about money. But the most we ever ask is a tithe, 10 percent. Most members don't do that. It's too much, we think, with all the other demands on our resources. So we start saying, "Just give what you can. Start out at 1 percent and work your way up." We try to make sacrifice as painless as we can. Now read Genesis 22, and the next time we see each other, you tell me if what we're doing is enough.

WHEN LIFE TAKES
THE UNEXPECTED TURN

Acts 4:23-24
Charles Bugg

C. S. Lewis, the well-known Christian writer, said, "There are times in all of our lives when the angels hold their breath to see which way we will go." If we've lived for any length of time, we know what Lewis is saying. Things are moving along well. The sun is shining. The future seems bright. Then the stabbing news comes—the diagnosis of the doctor, a child who is terribly ill, a job we lose, the terrible ripping of a relationship that seemed so secure.

What do we do? How do we respond? How easy it is to believe in God when we're basking in the brightness. How difficult it is when the brightness becomes a blur. The book of Acts tells us about a time in the life of the early church when "the angels were holding their breath." We read the first few chapters of Acts, and things couldn't be any better. The church was adding members, the fellowship among the members was pure, and if somebody in the church needed anything, others responded with generosity.

Even the reputation of the church in the community was wonderful. People who weren't even believers said the folks in the community of faith seem to be good people. Add to this the success of Peter's sermons. When we left Peter in the last part of Luke's Gospel, he had lost his voice. "I really don't know him," he told the slave girl as he slithered into the darkness before Jesus died. But in the second volume of Luke's history, who's front and center in the first part of Acts? Peter gives voice to the faith of these early believers, and thousands respond, "What shall we do?"

As a preacher, I've dreamed of a Sunday like that. Frankly, I don't really think Peter's sermon is that good. He recites a lot of Hebrew Bible, and then he tells his largely Jewish audience, "Jesus was the promised one." There are no cute stories, no clever phrases, nothing about children or animals—it's just Bible! I have some cute stories about children and a few cute dog and cat narratives. Some of these stories will make you cry, and some will make you laugh. Peter preaches the Bible, and of all things, thousands come forward on the invitation.

The preacher also needs to worship. So Peter and John go to the temple in Jerusalem to pray. It's three in the afternoon. A man who has been physically challenged since birth sees John and Peter and asks alms. "Silver and gold have we none, but such as we have we give you," the two men respond. Then they give him healing. "In Jesus' name," or as we may say, "by the power of Jesus," we tell you that what was broken is now made whole.

The healed man is ecstatic. He's shouting and praising and telling everyone that Peter and John changed him in the name of someone called Jesus. Here the whole flavor of the book of Acts changes. Up to now, the church has been tolerated. But now Peter and John have crossed the line. Persecution replaces acceptance. Brought before the authorities, these two are jailed, admonished, and told no more healing in Jesus' name and no more talk of a Savior raised from the dead.

Of course, that's the heart of the church's message. On the third day, Jesus was raised, and the church lives, moves, and has its being in the power and name of the risen Lord. The authorities say no more. John and Peter reply we must keep saying and doing the message. The disciples leave and return to the rest of the church.

Here is the critical moment. What will the church do? The church is still the people of Pentecost, but they are now people who will be tracked, followed, and persecuted. Do you think angels were holding their breath? It's nice when God loves you, you love God, people love you, and all's right in heaven and on earth. That kind of faith attracts me. Why not be "appropriately" religious? If we have to lower our voices as the church, then let's do that so everybody is happy. Surely God understands. We have to go along to get along. Why be concerned about the physically or mentally challenged? Sure, a lot of people who are struggling emotionally can't afford medication because most health management companies see a broken arm as a worthier cause than a broken spirit. Sure, the streets of our inner cities are filled at night with homeless people, many of them mentally challenged. What's the reasoning? If somebody is really strong, he will help himself. Just get over it. Get a job and make a living like the rest of us. Ministers may really get themselves in trouble if they tell some folks in the church that these people on the streets and sleeping in cardboard boxes can't make it without their help.

Thank God Peter and John didn't tell the authorities, "We'll go along to get along." What they did say was, "We can't help but speak about the things we've seen and heard." Sometimes truth is more important than consequences. The two followers of Jesus return to the church. Things are different now. The authorities tolerated us, but now they will track us down. Before, we could preach and tell people our story. We could praise our God and say that Jesus of Nazareth is the anointed one. Now, we are the enemy, the hunted ones. They told us to be quiet, but we can't. We've seen and heard something that has changed our very beings. The church now persecuted comes together, and what do they do?

They pray. The church bows heads together and remembers an old Jewish prayer about Elohim, God. "Sovereign Lord, you made the heavens and the earth and the sea, and everything in them." Then the church remembers a psalm about how the rulers and authorities raged against the anointed one of Saul.

The church prayed, "Elohim," you who made everything. I'm glad the church stayed together and prayed. When things go badly, we may panic, we may run, we may become cynical, bitter, our teeth set on edge. We may long for simpler times. Who hasn't pressed her face against the window on the fourth day of rain and longed for a glimpse of the sun. I have to commend the early church—they prayed.

It's what they prayed that seems a little strange. When you and I are in difficulty, we know what to pray. We pray for rescue; we pray for relief; we pray for strength. But the church in Acts didn't ask for anything. They remembered that God had made everything.

I know the doctrine of creation divides people. Some people say the creation story is literal truth. In fact, an Archbishop Usher said everything started in 4004 BC. Forget evolution. Forget the fossils. Forget the dinosaurs. Forget the exploding stars that indicate creation is still happening. According to some, the test of faith is whether you and I believe that Adam and Eve were literal people.

Too bad or maybe too good that the early church understood creation in a different way. To people whose lives have been radically changed, what matters is there's a God who has made all of creation in whatever way God chooses. Because what really, really matters is that God made it, God loves it, and God is still in control.

Sure, life has pain. Let's not kid ourselves. You and I both know that since we came to faith in Jesus Christ, life hasn't been one wonderful event after another. Yet, what if we believe that life is ultimately chaos—that nothing or nobody is in control and everything that happens is random.

The church chooses a different road. If they'd chosen the road called random, I don't believe the community would have made it. We may practice random acts of kindness, but are our lives just a series of random acts? What do Peter, John, and the other followers do? They remember. They remember a prayer. It's the prayer they need. Life changes, and the community of faith bows their heads. "God you made us; we are in your hands."